Lynda T. Tolton
Fitzwilliam
Community Church

The First Year Alone

D1569217

Beverly S. Gordon

THE
FIRST YEAR
ALONE

Foreword by Elizabeth Yates

William L. Bauhan, Publisher
DUBLIN, NEW HAMPSHIRE

Copyright © 1986 by Beverly S. Gordon
All Rights Reserved
Library of Congress Cataloguing in Publication data:
Gordon, Beverly S., 1931-
The first year alone.
Bibliography: p.
1. Bereavement. 2. Grief. 3. Gordon, Beverly S.
1931-   . I. Title.
BJ1487.G67 1986   155.9'37   85-13557
ISBN 0-87233-082-6

While the incidents related in this book are absolutely factual, in some cases fictitious names have been substituted to protect true identities.

Grateful acknowledgment is made for quotations used in this book from: *Sunrise*, White Eagle Publishing Trust, Liss, Hampshire, England, 1958; *My God, My God!* by Ruth Vaughn, © 1982 by Impact Books, by permission of the Zondervan Corporation, Grand Rapids, Michigan; and *On That Night* by Elizabeth Yates, E.P. Dutton, New York, 1969.

Published 1986 by William L. Bauhan, Publisher, Old County Road, Dublin, N.H. 03444

Printed in the United States of America.

First Printing, March 1986
Second Printing, October 1986

For Tom

A Word to the Reader

WHEN TOM GORDON DIED—suddenly but not unexpectedly—of a heart attack, the question asked by those who knew them was, "*What* will Beverly do?" This book is her answer.

Beverly and Tom Gordon had a wide circle of friends, among whom I was something of a latecomer, but before Tom died I had seen that they were uniquely well-suited, that they complemented each other in every conceivable way. Teaching had been a common bond from the start, and even when multiple sclerosis cut Beverly's career short, their interests remained similar and shared. Each stimulated and enriched the other—Beverly with the world of books and reading, Tom with gardening and beekeeping.

She had long been a journal keeper and so she continued after Tom's death, recording events that were bewildering and agonizing as day followed day, and the thoughts and emotions that accompanied the events. After some months she began to realize that fully important as the events, were the discoveries she was making. Gradually, oh so gradually, something was happening. Something buoyed, then strengthened and set her on a forward course. Call it wisdom, perhaps. Like Isolt in Edward Arlington Robinson's *Tristram*, she could say—

Wisdom is like a dawn that comes up slowly
Out of an unknown ocean.

A time of grieving had become a year of growing.

One day she asked me if I would care to read her journal and tell her if there was anything in it that might have meaning for others. She knew she had gone over a road that many must travel at some time and the milestones passed were common to all. Keeping a diary had been a refuge; reading over it, one could see how she had grown. Faced by a challenge, she had accepted it and found a way to live again; that living would be within the limits imposed by her wheelchair, but she could develop skill as a writer and with her words reach out. This would be her gift to others and giving it she would honor the love she and Tom had known.

And so I read, often with difficulty, as the early pages were blotted with the tears that in her first grief fell so uncontrollably.

What came through with persuasive force was that Beverly, the teacher, had been teaching herself. She did not attempt to tell others what to do or how to do it; she recorded what she had done: facing the demands of practical everyday tasks that linked her with others; learning to accept the support of caring friends, books read, thoughts that eased the long nights when sleep was a stranger. I saw in the words crowding the pages that Beverly was learning to let love happen in her life again. In the first bleakness she had felt cut off, but now no longer.

8

It was not love such as she and Tom had known, but it was love that was comforting, refreshing, and to which she could respond.

She had asked me a question. My answer to her was "Yes."

Often we tend to think of people who have met and come through grievous trials as gallant and courageous, but Beverly has gone beyond that. Her ever-widening circle of friends forget the courage and the gallantry and see her as one who has found a richness in living that she is ready to share.

ELIZABETH YATES

Looking Back

TOM WAS SELDOM MOODY, so the day he came home noticeably quiet after having an annual physical checkup, I expressed wifely concern. "Is something wrong?" I asked.

Handing me a bottle of prescribed medication with a label that read FOR HYPERTENSION, Tom gently explained. "My blood pressure is a little on the high side. Dr. Ramsay says it's borderline, nothing to worry about, and probably most doctors would not even bother to treat it. He's just being cautious, Hon."

Tom had dismissed the matter lightly, but I was not fooled. I was convinced that his casual manner was only a mask and that he was worried and frightened. It was not until bedtime, however, that he was ready to admit the truth and to share his real feelings.

How valid was the medical theory that heart disease might be hereditary? he wondered. His paternal grandparents and his father had died of it. "But more than that, I'm angry at my body," Tom confessed. "Can you understand?"

I squeezed his hand tenderly and reminded him that I understood well. And I did. After all, I had experienced that kind of anger myself some years earlier when a neurologist had finally sorted out a bizarre and puzzling set of symptoms that added up to multiple sclerosis. Tom and I were just beginning to give serious thought to having a family. MS made the decision for us. We were told there was no known cure for the disease, which affected different parts of the central nervous system and usually ran an unpredictable course. We chose not to raise a child under those circumstances.

Multiple sclerosis had changed our lives; hypertension would not, I assured Tom on that day when he came home with his prescription. And I believed my own words. Yes, we would move through the years on our hilltop in Peterborough, New Hampshire, in the wood-shingled, one-story house Tom and I had carefully planned together. A view of Temple Mountain and Pack Monadnock across the valley and Mount Monadnock to the west, along with open fields, stone walls, and surrounding woods, gave us the sense of country living we both loved. Tom would someday retire from teaching physics at Conval, the Contoocook Valley Regional High School, and give his energies instead to the small apple orchard he had planted in our backyard, to the garden he loved, and to his beekeeping. I would share in it all vicariously and perhaps even give more time to a newfound interest in writing. There was still much ahead for us. It was that simple.

But I was wrong. Eight years after I assured Tom that our lives would not change because of borderline hypertension, he suffered two massive heart attacks within nine months and died of the second one at age forty-seven.

The obituary notice in the newspaper used the phrase "survivors include," and my name appeared first in the list of close relatives. A question sprang immediately into my mind: How could the word "survivor" in any way be connected to me? Didn't it mean continuing to live after or in spite of some disaster, such as a shipwreck? I did not feel like a survivor. I was deep in the wreckage. I was drowning. The dearest, the best, the most important person in my life had been torn from me. How was I going to go on living after or in spite of that?

I had not the slightest idea. All I knew was that one afternoon my husband had suddenly dismissed students from his classroom and driven himself to the hospital because of severe chest pain, and ten days later I was a widow. The roughest, steepest road I had ever traveled lay ahead. This book is a record of my journey.

The First Year Alone

I

Acceptance of what has happened is the first step to overcoming the consequences of any misfortune.

— WILLIAM JAMES

APRIL 9

TOM CALLED FROM THE HOSPITAL early this morning. His voice sounded strange. It was steady, but high-pitched and with a strained quality, as if his throat was tight and he was forcing every word from it.

"I'm back in intensive care," he said. "They are setting up IVs and things."

"Yes, I know. I just talked to the floor nurse. Ferris is here loading my wheelchair into the car. I'm on my way."

"I love you, Hon. Good-by."

"I love you, too. I'll see you in a few minutes."

I was glad to have Ferris with me. As a friend she offered loving support, and as a professional relaxation therapist she practiced what she preached. Her cool manner was instantly contagious. If she was worried, it didn't show. Her eyes were as blue and bright as always, and there was the usual quick, easy smile.

When we arrived at the hospital, Janet was standing

inside the entrance door. I didn't think there was anything out of the ordinary about her being there. After all, she was a medical secretary at the hospital and a friend of Ferris's and mine.

"We're on our way upstairs to see Tom," I said. "How about leading the way?"

Janet gave me a big, motherly hug, glanced at Ferris, then gripped the arm of my wheelchair so strongly that I could not move on. I looked at her. The color had drained from her face and her dark eyes showed a fear that I had never seen before.

"I think we had better go into the Quiet Room," Janet said. "You can't see Tom right now. The doctors are working on him."

A scream came from somewhere inside me. The sound startled me and ushered in a flood of thoughts. The Quiet Room. O God, no! I had wheeled past there dozens of times. It was near the physical therapy room where I went for treatments, and I knew it was the special place where families waited for word of the condition of a patient who was seriously injured or in crisis. Oh, God, now it was my turn.

Dr. Forssell appeared for a moment. Calm and serious, he looked directly at me, wasting no words. "Tom has gone into cardiac arrest. He is in bad shape."

Ferris, Janet, and I sat in that close, windowless room, holding hands, taking deep, full breaths. We prayed—sometimes aloud together, sometimes silently, each in her own way. But nothing eased my terror. My stomach churned, the back of my neck tightened, my head pounded, my heart raced. Through tears, I shouted at Tom. "Hold on. Pull through. Live!" I shouted at God, too. "Please don't take Tom away from me. Don't let him die."

Ferris helped me out of my wheelchair and onto a couch. She had tucked her long red hair behind her ears and her face, like Janet's, was ashen.

A nurse came in and held my hand. "Is Tom going to make it?" I asked.

"I don't know, Bev." The reply was an honest one.

The door opened. I turned and looked at Dr. Forssell. He seemed unable to speak the words, so I did it for him. "Tom is gone."

Dr. Forssell bent down and kissed my forehead. "I'm so sorry, Bev. Tom's heart just couldn't beat anymore."

Numbness, shock, disbelief, despair.

I refused the offer to view Tom's body. "It is only his body," I said. "His spirit has left it. I want to remember him alive, not dead." But when asked about an autopsy, I said yes. Something within demands an answer, a reason, an explanation.

My way of dealing with stress has always been to keep busy, and it was no different today. As soon as I got home, I stretched out on the bed and reached for the telephone. There were so many people to call, and I wanted to do it myself. Somehow, hearing my own voice saying the words, "Tom died this morning," over and over again had a numbing effect and seemed to shut out any denial of what had happened.

Calls to the family and the high school came first, and they were the hardest. Then I faced a long list of friends.

Elizabeth said, "Oh, Beverly, just think — today is Good Friday." I thought about it after I hung up the phone. Yes, Good Friday, the day Christ died on the cross for our sins that we might have life everlasting. It did not console me. Nothing does. All expressions of sympathy, no matter how heartfelt, seem empty to me today. Tom is dead, and the hurt inside me cannot be eased by gentle words or anything else.

APRIL 10

I have no recollection of eating supper or getting into bed last night. I only remember feeling emotionally, mentally, and physically drained from grief and worn out from talking to people who were kind enough to telephone or come by in person.

Mary spent the night. Of those who offered to stay, she was the one I wanted to have with me. Beyond our close friendship, we now share a common bond—widowhood. It is only five years since Mary lost Russell and, like Tom, Russell died at a young age of heart disease. I knew Mary would understand my anguish.

Exhausted as I was, sleep came no more than two or three hours at a time. In between, I cried. (Thank God, Mary never once said, "You must stop crying."). I feared silence, darkness, being alone in my room, and I asked that the hall light and the radio be left on.

Mary slept curled up under a blanket in Tom's easy chair next to my bed. I doubt that she got much rest. Sometime during the night she was in the kitchen fixing a cup of warm milk for me, remembering how that simple remedy had helped her sleep in the first weeks after Russell died. I sat up in bed and sipped the milk while Mary leaned back in the chair, took off her glasses, and closed her eyes. She looked small in the oversized chair, and her prematurely white hair stood out against the orange fabric.

The funeral director was here today to pick up clothes

for Tom to wear in his casket and to talk over plans for a service. It seemed unbearable and yet I know it must be done. It is the beginning of good-by.

Tom and I once discussed our feelings concerning funerals. He said that if I should ever have to plan his, I was to make it simple and do whatever was easiest for me, and so I did.

There will be a private memorial service. I have requested that in lieu of flowers, donations may be made to a scholarship fund I am establishing in Tom's name at the high school. It seems right. As a teacher, Tom valued education, was dedicated to his profession, and was respected by his students. But more than that, there is a redeeming aspect to the scholarship idea. If Tom had to die so young, while he still had much to give to high-school science students, I want it to count for something.

APRIL 11. EASTER SUNDAY

Norma has a few days off from her live-in nurse-companion job across town, so she is spending them with me. I don't think we have ever felt closer as sisters. When she came in late last evening, we cried together, shared memories of Tom, and talked until we were exhausted and finally gave in to much-needed sleep. We were awake at dawn this Easter morning. While the sun came up over the mountains and filled the east window of my room with light, Norma read aloud from a book Mary gave to me called *Sunrise*.

The book is about life beyond death as revealed to a medium from a spiritual teacher whose pseudonym is "White Eagle." It spoke of the resurrection of Jesus and the enduring peace of God.

Learn so to love God that you know that God, being Himself all love, and having all love for you, has in Him no death, but only a more abundant life. Your loved one dwells within that Love, and also within your own spirit. He is therefore with you, not lost, not gone far away.

Try never to think of anyone as being 'dead.' Think of them as living more abundantly in a land which you know they would love; and please, not as living idly; idleness they would not find inspiring. Wherever their heart inclines them they will find their work, and work to their heart's content.

I visualized Tom and saw him clearly. His tall, trim figure moved with sureness through a place of beauty, light, and tranquility; his hazel eyes were no longer clouded by pain or medication, and the gray streak I used to tease him about still looked distinctly set apart from his otherwise brown hair.

It eased my sorrow, but only for a little while.

APRIL 12

Norma took me to the cemetery today because I had to choose a burial plot. I wish I could have spared her the agony of it. She is taking Tom's death very hard, and it shows. Pencil thin to begin with, she looks more fragile than ever, and there are dark circles under her eyes.

The funeral director met us at the cemetery. Politely and considerately, he showed us what was available, told us the cost, and stressed how pleasant the surroundings were. It all seemed unreal. I felt as if I were outside my body watching someone else who looked exactly like me. The funeral director's lips were moving, but my mind grasped only a few words—*grave, perpetual care, marker*. I wanted to run away. I didn't belong there.

Suddenly, I pointed to a plot and said, "This one will be fine."

"That's Number 6 Cedar Avenue," the funeral director replied. "I'll make arrangements to have the deed mailed to you in a few days."

As we drove away, I cried. All I could think of was that Tom now has a new address — 6 Cedar Avenue. He will be there; I'll be somewhere else. By the time I got home, I felt totally separated from him.

The Support Group met here this evening. It was a tribute to Tom and a time for looking back. Ferris, as our counselor, took the lead and reminded us of how we first came together six months ago as a small gathering of people learning to cope with various long-term illnesses and seeking to share feelings and give support to each other. Someone spoke of what a lot of sorrow we have suffered in a short period of time. With Tom's death, we have now lost two of our original six members.

I value these special friends, who became an important part of my life and Tom's soon after his first heart attack. The word "support" has more meaning to me than ever before. I know that dealing with my grief is going to take enormous courage on my part, and I shall need help from others. I need to share the pain and suffering. I need to talk about my feelings of anger, abandonment, and hopelessness. I need love, understanding, and reassurance.

APRIL 13

The memorial service was held today at the funeral home. It was brief and simple; prayers, psalms, a few words read by Dana Horrell, the minister. I was there in body but not in spirit. While I realize that society dictates that we need an appointed time, place, and manner in which to say good-by to someone who has died, today's service did not fill that purpose for me.

Family and friends came to the house afterward. I was so depleted of energy that I had to lie down, and one by one, people came into my room to sit and talk for a few minutes. My heart crumbled when Tom's mother came in. Tom is the third grown child she has lost, and her only son. We clung to each other and wept, then she held my hand and asked again and again, "Why did Tom have to die?" It is a question I keep asking, too, and I have no answer.

APRIL 16

There is no time to write in my journal on a daily basis. I am in a whirl of activity to get my life organized. I don't know where the energy is coming from, since I sleep no more than four hours a night and am eating very little.

Putting first things first, I have worked out a way to manage the day-to-day routine. Two different people take turns spending the night, then in the morning a home health aide from the Visiting Nurse Association arrives to fix breakfast, help me get dressed, make the bed, and put a cold lunch in the refrigerator before leaving so that I can wheel out to the kitchen and have something to eat at noon. Mother and Dad come in about five o'clock to cook supper.

But it is all temporary, and my life seems uncertain.

Looking at finances, it is clear that I cannot afford to hire a full-time housekeeper. I think the thing to do is to search for someone who would be willing to live in and give me the limited help I need in exchange for free room and board. I don't know how to begin except to spread the word among family and friends as to what I have in mind and hope that an idea will surface.

During the daytime, friends come and go. I can especially count on seeing Mary every day late in the afternoon when she is free from her teacher's aide job at Conval. It is the same with Janet, who seldom fails to stop by on her way home from working at the hospital. I welcome all the company that flows through my door, but am keenly aware that it will dwindle as time goes on. I cannot expect people to continue to put aside their own busy lives and spend "hand-holding" hours with me.

When I am alone, I am occupied with paperwork. There are thank-you notes to write. Forms must be filled out for insurance claims, social security, and the teachers' retirement fund so that I will not be without money to pay the bills.

Yesterday Norma helped me clean out the bedroom closet and some bureau drawers. I cannot bear the sight of Tom's clothes—the trousers, neckties, cardigans, and white shirts he wore to work, the Irish tweed hat I gave him one Christmas, the sweaters his mother knit for him, all seem like ghosts to me now.

I was all right until we got to the shoes, then I fell apart. Tom's feet should be in those shoes, I thought—the highly polished ones for school, the scuffed-up boots for garden and yard chores, the slippers for evenings at home. Yes, Tom should be wearing all those shoes for all those reasons. But he isn't.

Within two hours everything, except one sweater I want to keep, was packed up and on its way to an institution where people desperately need clothing. As with the schol-

25

arship idea, I am thinking of redemption. If Tom had to die, it must count for something. His clothes must be put to use.

To dispose of Tom's things is a necessary part of the good-by, the severing, the letting go, but it hurts. I feel as if I am wounding Tom in a personal way, bit by bit throwing away pieces of the person I loved most in my life.

APRIL 18

George telephoned this morning to remind me that as a neighbor and friend, he is standing by with a helping hand whenever I need it. Something came to mind at once.

While Tom was in the hospital, his thoughts were often of home, and one day he asked me to find someone to check the apple trees in the backyard. "There may be some mice damage," he said. "I don't want my trees to die, Hon."

I could not find anyone then, but now I asked George if he would like to inspect the orchard. His immediate "yes" did not surprise me. A gardener for most of his seventy years, he loves anything to do with nature and growing things.

George came by later today to explain in his usual patient way that one or two trees are in sad condition but can probably be saved by a process of bridging and grafting. "I wondered where I was going to get the scions for the job," he said, "and when I was walking cross lots up to your house just now, the darnedest thing happened. As I passed near the edge of the woods, the branch of a wild apple tree caught my sleeve. I looked up at it and said, 'Well now, old fellow, what do you want?' I think that branch was trying to tell me something, don't you, Bev?"

I could only nod my head speechlessly and wonder about the possible nearness of Tom's spirit, as George did.

APRIL 23

Friends are important in these days of despair. Even those who are far away and can reach out only through letters are offering love and support, and I treasure their words of caring.

A letter from Emily says, "Because my beloved parents and my closest woman friend have gone, I think I know a bit about loss through death. But surely losing a husband is different from that and is, perhaps, the worst kind of sorrow."

Emily is right, and the reason (for me, at least) is that Tom was my husband, my lover, and my best friend all in one. That adds up to a triple loss. No wonder the grief is so deep.

Emily also writes of my being in a little boat "entering a dark, fearful gulf. I pray that God will be in the little boat with you," she says. "Thus you are safe, never alone."

I wish I had a sense of God being with me, but I have not yet learned to cast out worry, doubt, and fear and replace it with complete trust in Him. I find myself easily slipping away from my companion in "the little boat" Emily speaks of.

Connie has written to say, "I am sure the love and concern of friends can carry one through each day on the surface, but nothing can reach deep down and heal that terrible ache you must be feeling."

The words ring true. Sometimes I think I am actually drawing a kind of energy from the loving support that is around me. It keeps me going, and yes, a degree of soothing comfort comes from it, but my pain has not eased.

It is like having immediate care for a deep cut. While stitches can be taken and medication can be given so that you can begin to function all right, beneath the doctor's careful work and beyond any temporary relief that medication brings, there is still the wound itself, and the healing has to take place.

MAY 7

My search for someone to live in has finally ended, in an unexpected way.

I telephoned the dentist's office one day last week to reschedule an appointment, and the hygienist asked how I was managing at home without Tom. When I told Anita of my search for someone to live in, she offered to get in touch with a nurse friend of hers at the Crotched Mountain Rehabilitation Center in Greenfield, a dozen miles north. "One of the employees might be looking for a place to live," Anita said.

I didn't think anything would come of it, but two days ago Anita called back to say that she had talked with her friend and was sending someone over to meet me. I interviewed Debbie Moreshead, a Maine native who is presently a nurse's aide at Crotched but plans to go to nursing school starting late August. Debbie's references were excellent, and I liked her at once. She struck me as a nice combination of someone who is physically strong, capable, self-confident and at the same time easygoing and sensitive. And she loves to cook!

Debbie moved in this afternoon, and I feel relieved. This buys me some three months of time to look for a more permanent live-in companion and releases all the people who have been helping me these past weeks. (Except for the home health aide who will stay on because Debbie has to be at work by 6:00 A.M.).

When I thanked Mother for the suppers she cooked, she kissed my cheek and with tears in her eyes said, "I love you." That was a gift I shall never forget. By her own admission, Mother finds it difficult to be openly warm and affectionate. I cannot remember her ever saying "I love you" to me before.

Debbie's moving in meant some rearranging of furniture. Tom's chair, his reading lamp, and the bench where he kept his books and magazines have been removed from the bedroom to allow space for my desk and file cabinet that were in the den where Debbie will now sleep. It was yet another uprooting and change, and my tears flowed.

Ferris stopped by after everything was in place. "This really looks like *your* room now," she said.

Dear God, how true! There is no more "our" room or "our" anything. Life is no longer in terms of *us* or *we*. I wonder if I shall ever get used to it.

MAY 8

I am hungry for even the smallest bit of information about Tom's last days. Because Ferris had visited him several times while he was hospitalized, I asked her yesterday if there was anything she could tell me.

She recalled going into Tom's room one day when there was a snowstorm. She found Tom looking out the window and weeping. "I've been lying here thinking that this is probably the last time I'll ever see it snow," he said.

So Tom knew he was not going to live. He kept it well

hidden from me. I talked to him on the telephone every day while he was in the hospital, and he was always cheerful and optimistic.

Ferris says that I must remember that Tom had to let go of me just as much as I am now having to let go of him. He didn't want to do it. By not sharing with me his thoughts of death, he was resisting the idea of leaving me. He could speak of it to others, but not to me.

MAY 10

The home health aide accidentally took the bifold closet door off its track this morning when she was getting a sweater for me. She didn't know how to fix it, and I told her not to be concerned about it. After she left, however, I nearly went off the track myself.

I was alone in the house and suddenly started to shout at the walls: "Who is going to fix things? There is no husband here anymore. The house will fall down around me!"

It was the same way the day I discovered some water on the floor near a radiator in the laundry room. "It's nothing to worry about," Dad said.

"But I *am* worried," I screamed at the walls after Dad left. "What if I ignore the leak and the floor rots? What if a pipe should burst?"

When things need to be repaired, I become more aware of my aloneness. Tom and I shared the responsibilities of running the house, but now he is gone, and my role is a dual one. I am not ready to take on so much all at once.

MAY 18

Ferris drove me to Boston today to keep an appointment I had made with a neurologist some weeks before Tom died. It was for a routine reevaluation of my MS, and I could easily have canceled it, but I felt that if I stayed home I would be breaking a promise to Tom. I couldn't do that.

A girl in the doctor's office was filling out a form with my name on it. "Next of kin?" she asked.

I couldn't speak. My mind simply went blank. Tom had always been my "next of kin." Finally Ferris said, "How about me, Bev?"

"Yes, fine."

"Your relationship?" the girl at the desk asked.

"Friend," Ferris replied.

Then the girl went on to the next question. "What is your marital status, Beverly?"

"Widow."

It was the first time I had said that word out loud since Tom's death. It sounded foreign and didn't seem to suit me any more than a purple dress with sequins would. I was happier and more comfortable with the title "wife."

MAY 21

Every morning lately I hear a cardinal singing at daybreak. I smile and tell myself that it is Tom saying good morning. Of course I know it isn't, but I like to think of it in that way, just as I like to think that the apple tree branch that caught at George's sleeve might have been Tom's spirit. It is comforting.

Each day, Tom seems farther and farther away, and I feel a deep need to "connect" to him through something tangible, like the bird and the tree branch. And today the man who bought Tom's beehive said he would like to keep it here in the backyard where Tom had it. He can't know how happy that makes me. It is like having a small part of Tom close by.

But the tangible connection can bring pain too.

It was cold this evening, and I decided to wear Tom's sweater. I pulled the sweater over my head, then found it uncomfortably big, and started to take it off. Suddenly, the odor of something familiar made my heart race. It was simply Tom. That special odor of just him, sweet and clean. I buried my face in the sweater, taking deep breaths to bring Tom closer, while at the same time I was sobbing with the pain of missing him.

I doubt that I shall ever wear that sweater—it doesn't fit. And yet I am not ready to give it away. There may be times when I'll want to bury my face in it again.

MAY 23

Weekends are rough. I feel especially lonely then because friends do not drop in as they do on weekdays. They are with husbands and families, and that is as it should be, but I feel left out.

I try to fill the hours by writing letters, reading, and watching television, but nothing takes me out of a restless, depressed mood once it settles in on me.

This was Debbie's Sunday to work, and the house was so quiet and empty that by late afternoon I thought I couldn't stand it another minute. I pounded my fists on the bed, crying, "Tom, Tom!" and then sobbed until I fell asleep. An hour later I woke up, still in a black mood. All I could think of was the days, months, and years ahead without Tom. It overwhelmed me.

I called Mary, and she was dear enough to let me pour my heart out to her on the telephone. "I know I should take one day at a time," I said, "but I can't seem to do it."

"On the bad days that's too much," Mary said. "Ask

God to get you through one hour, or even just five minutes, at a time. That's what I did in the early months after Russell died."

I felt better after talking to Mary, but I wouldn't want her to know how much courage it took for me to call her today. I picked up the phone twice before I actually dialed her number. I don't want to be a nuisance to my friends.

MAY 26

The school principal telephoned this morning to give me the name of a young man who is to receive the Thomas K. Gordon Memorial Scholarship this year.

"Where will he be going to college?" I asked.

"Rensselaer Polytechnic Institute," came the reply.

I could hardly believe my ears. RPI—Tom's alma mater! I don't know of any student from the local high school who has ever gone to that college. "Why this year?" I have asked myself a hundred times today.

I am pleased that the award went to someone who will walk the same campus Tom once walked and perhaps sit in some of the same classrooms where he sat. This tells me how right it was to establish the scholarship.

MAY 31

Yesterday Norma took me to the cemetery to put flowers on Tom's grave for Memorial Day. We had trouble figuring out which plot was his because the marker is not yet in place. Finally we found a small metal tab with a 6 on it that had been pounded into the ground.

I had hoped that visiting the grave would comfort me, but it didn't. I came home feeling more separated from Tom than ever.

Last night I dreamed of Tom for the first time since he died. In the dream, I was trying to scream, but nothing would come out. I woke myself crying, "Help me, help me!" Then for a split second I saw Tom standing at the foot of the bed. It was all so real and at the same time almost mystical.

This morning Debbie said something disturbed her during the night. She listened for a minute to see if I was calling her, but heard nothing and went back to sleep.

JUNE 2

Connie and Nat have returned from their trip to Wales and telephoned this morning to set a time for coming to see me. After I hung up the phone, I thought of what dear people they are—Connie in her role as friend and surrogate big sister to me and Nat like a favorite uncle. I waited for them at the door. When they arrived how happy I was to see those two familiar tall, thin figures get out of the car and walk toward me!

Our reunion was an emotional one, as I knew it would be. When Connie and Nat left last March to spend three months with their daughter and grandchildren, in Wales, all was well. There was no reason to believe they would never see Tom again.

I was telling Connie about going to the cemetery and how meaningless I find it. "But Bev, Tom has never really been there," she reminded me.

I hadn't thought of that before. The last place that Tom *was* was in the hospital. That is where his spirit separated from his body. All that the cemetery holds is his shell. The part of him that lives on is not buried in the ground, it is free and spiritual. If I can just remember that, maybe it will be less painful to visit his grave.

34

JUNE 4

Today I found myself thinking about the night before Tom went to the hospital. I heard him stirring around in the kitchen, then he came back to bed.

"Are you all right?" I asked.

He told me his chest was uncomfortable and that he had taken a nitroglycerine pill.

"Why didn't you wake me?" I said.

Tom's eyes filled with tears. "I didn't want to, Hon. I sat on the edge of the bed for a while watching you sleep and thinking how much I love you."

We held each other and cried together for a few minutes, then I gently rubbed Tom's back and shoulders. He went to sleep at once.

How lucky I was to have known the kind of love and devotion that Tom gave me! I keep asking myself why he had to die. I know of husbands who are hopeless alcoholics, husbands who beat their wives, husbands who are unfaithful. Why couldn't they have been the ones to die?

JUNE 6

Everyone is generous with advice, and I wish they wouldn't be. It only confuses me. So I have hired a lawyer to help with some details of settling Tom's estate that I do not feel competent enough to handle myself. Now when well-meaning friends and relatives say, "You should do this," or "You shouldn't do that," I simply reply with, "My lawyer is handling that matter for me." It is amazing how quickly that phrase has put an end to the advice giving, except for Aunt Anna, "Lawyers are expensive," she said.

"There is no reason in the world why you can't take care of everything yourself."

I didn't even try to defend myself. I have to learn to trust my own judgment, and I might as well start now.

Everyone tells me it is best for widows not to make big decisions right away, but surely it was wise for me to start getting my finances in order at once. Checks for insurance claims are in, and I have talked with a financial adviser about investing the money. It eases the worry of how I am going to pay the bills that are on my desk.

But what seems even more important is this: With so much paperwork behind me, I feel as if I have taken the first step on a long journey that lies ahead. Fact is fact. My life has changed, and I must reorganize every part of it.

JUNE 9

I am still cleaning out closets and bureau drawers. It seems essential if I am to think in terms of beginning anew. Certainly as I have moved through various stages of my life—high school to college, college to a job, single life to marriage—I parted with things that were no longer needed. Now, as a widow, I must do the same.

It is painful to sort out all of Tom's belongings. Each is a stinging reminder of his absence, and each stirs thoughts of him. Today I found a pocket-size copy of the New Testament with an inscription at the front that tells me the book was given to Tom at age ten by his Sunday school teacher. It set me to thinking about Tom's attitude toward God.

Although he was brought up in a Christian home, years later Tom questioned the existence of God. He said science got in the way. As a physics teacher, he thought there was a scientific explanation for everything. He simply could not accept the idea of some invisible "being" so powerful as to create the world. "Besides," he confessed one day, "when we found out about your multiple sclerosis, I asked God to heal you, and nothing happened."

Tom did believe in Christ, however, and even if his belief was strictly on his own terms, I am at peace with it. He thought of Christ not as the Son of God, but as a wise philosopher who tried to teach the meaning of love and the right way to live.

Surely if God is all that I believe Him to be, I need not worry about any of this. I think He knows the goodness of Tom's heart and holds him in His loving arms.

JUNE 11

The legal details of settling Tom's estate seem endless, and yet I am glad to be busy with it. It gives me a reason to get up in the morning and forces me to function. The family thinks I am doing too much and getting overtired, but I can't tell them my secret fear.

I don't want to lose my mind.

I am haunted by a story Tom told me years ago of a woman whose husband died suddenly of a heart attack. "The day after the funeral, someone found Mrs. Tenison wandering around in the village, confused and naked," Tom said. I know the woman was elderly and that everyone handles stress differently, but my fear of going to pieces is real. My way of dealing with it is the busyness I allow myself to get caught up in.

Sometimes the grief is so deep it nearly swallows me, and I truly do wonder if I am going to hold together. Connie was here for a while this morning, but I was alone for lunch and as far as I knew, I would be alone until Debbie came home from work. I was busy with paperwork when suddenly I started to cry uncontrollably. I begged God to let me die. That was all I could think of. If I could just die, then I would be with Tom, and this terrible pain would go away forever.

My thoughts were so negative and filled with such self-destruction that it was frightening.

Then the doorbell rang, and Muriel walked in. "I thought I'd just stop by and see how you are doing," she said.

I don't know Muriel very well and felt embarrassed to have her find me crying and upset. But she was not uncomfortable with my tears. She gave me a hug, handed me some tissues, and talked quietly with me until I was all right again. I suppose that as the mother of seven children Muriel is used to doing all that, and I was grateful for the way she understood my desperate need for a little mothering.

After Muriel left, I decided that I am expecting too much of myself too soon. I should remember to ask God to help me get through one hour, or even five minutes at a time, as Mary suggested.

And I learned another lesson today.

I forgot God, but He didn't forget me. Surely it was not just a coincidence that Muriel rang the doorbell when I was feeling so desperate. Someone is watching over me and sending comfort when I need it. How can I doubt it?

JUNE 13

I have been surprised at not having a telephone call or a visit from Alison or Kate. As long-time friends they sent cards, but signed their names without any personal messages, and that seemed cold. I wish they knew how much I need to share my pain, how fragile I feel, and how I want the world to be tender with me.

It reminds me of my first homecoming from the hospital after the MS diagnosis. I needed a great deal of support to face what was ahead, and when people stayed away it hurt. In the beginning I rationalized that my friends cared so much about me that they couldn't bear to be a part of my suffering. They found it easier to keep their distance. But in time I came to another conclusion.

Sometimes people look at someone else's misfortune and see themselves. "Oh, my God, that could happen to me," they think. Perhaps that is the case with Alison and Kate. They still have their husbands. Their world is turning as always, but they know in their hearts that it could stop as abruptly as mine did.

I can't allow bitterness and self-pity to creep in on top of sorrow, however, and if some life-blasting event should touch the lives of those who have disappointed me, I would gladly offer my hand and heart to them. In all fairness, I must remember that those who have stayed away are balanced by those who have come forward—even in awkwardness.

One of Tom's colleagues from school stopped by today. I sensed his uneasiness, and finally he confessed it himself. "I have to tell you that I am uncomfortable about being here," Alec said. "I don't know what to say to you. I want to talk about Tom, but I'm not sure how you would feel about that."

I made an effort to put Alec at ease and assured him that talking about Tom would not disturb me in the least. On the contrary, I like to have people share their memories of Tom. It brings a warm feeling.

JUNE 14

Bob, one of Tom's students, was here this morning to tell me that the traditional senior class gift to the school will be made in honor of Tom this year. There will be two bronze plaques—one to name the physics room after Tom and to be placed at the entrance to the room; another to be placed in the room itself with these words: "This classroom and the lessons taught here are dedicated to the memory of Thomas K. Gordon, who spent eighteen years of his life teaching students about the wonders of our world."

It is an act of love, and as modest as Tom was, I think he would have been deeply touched by it, as I am. Thinking back to my own days as a teacher, I know that tributes have a special meaning when they are initiated by the students.

"The kids always came first with Mr. Gordon," Bob said as he reminisced about Tom. "I really think what he liked most was teaching. I loved the way he kept track of the moon, the planets, and the stars. Did you know he used to draw squares on his arm to explain barometric pressure?"

I knew, and could only smile and reach for a tissue. Then Bob went on to tell me something I *didn't* know. "Whenever there was an unanswerable 'why' question, Mr. Gordon would say, 'Because God wanted it that way.' "

I was startled. I have never heard Tom say anything like that. Perhaps he believed in God after all. I want to think that he did.

Without knowing it, Bob gave me a gift today.

JUNE 16

The tears have come like a waterfall all day. Why, I wonder, when yesterday was all right? Perhaps it is because we have had a long spell of rainy, gloomy weather, or because I don't feel well and Tom isn't here to boost my spirits as he always did when MS symptoms made me uncomfortable.

Last night, numbness in my arms and muscle spasms in my back kept me from sleeping. I needed some aspirin, and it took several calls before I could rouse Debbie to get it for me. When I finally settled down again, I reached out to the empty space in the bed and cried. Feeling alone and abandoned, I pulled Tom's pillow close to me and hugged it. I thought of the loving way he always took care of me and how I shall miss that the rest of my life.

JUNE 19

Connie invited me to spend a few hours with her and Nat today at their house. She thought a change of scenery would cheer me up. I wanted to go but felt guilty because I know how busy Connie and Nat are with getting things in order after being away for such a long time on their trip. I explained that to Connie, but she argued with me in a friendly way. Finally we made a compromise. I would sit on Connie's porch while she weeded her flower beds and Nat mowed the lawn, then we would all come together later for apple juice and crackers.

We left my wheelchair behind and with my cane and Connie's help, I walked the few steps to the car and later onto the porch. It tired me and brought an awareness of how much the stress of Tom's death has adversely affected my problems with multiple sclerosis, especially in the areas of stamina and balance. Still, it felt good to be in the sunshine and fresh air. I especially liked sitting on the porch where I could watch the birds in the apple tree, see the flowers that respond so well to Connie's green thumb, and gaze across the wide meadow that stretches out in front of the house.

But something strange happened when Connie and Nat joined me. It was an effort to concentrate on conversation, my thoughts kept wandering. I was so centered on Tom that for a while everything took on a dreamy, filmlike quality. Our voices, even my own, sounded far away.

When I came home, the house seemed as empty as my heart. I wanted Tom to be here, and after Connie left I cried. I wonder if I'll ever adjust to the fact that I am no longer part of a couple. No matter where I go or what I do, there is a feeling that half of me is missing.

JUNE 21

Last night was an evening of being alone and feeling my solitude—my solitariness—deeply. I should have found something to drive it away, but I didn't, and it was a mistake. Despair and hopelessness crept in and stayed with me, spilling over into today.

My world has been blown apart by Tom's death. I don't know how to come to terms with it. If I were well, it would be easier. I have dreamed about how I might spend my time. I would teach again, volunteer at the hospital on weekends, plant a garden, hike and bicycle in summer, ski in winter. But it is all fantasy, and I must find alternatives.

The one thing that takes me totally out of myself is writing. I want to get back to the half-written short story and unfinished poems that are tucked away in my file cabinet. The trouble is, I need long periods of uninterrupted time for it and that seems impossible to find in this period of trying to reorganize my life. Besides, my mind is in such a turmoil that I cannot think creatively. So for now, the only writing I shall do is in this journal. At least it keeps me putting words to paper.

In the loneliness of last night, I decided that I must draw myself completely into *now* and *future*. It is all right to keep *past* as if it were a box filled with treasures, and it is all right to look into the box once in a while, but it is wrong to dwell in it. And the treasures I choose to put into the box ought to be those that bring pleasure — memories of the happy times with Tom, not those of his illness and the last days of his life. The question is, can I do it?

July 3

I am home after being in the hospital with an MS attack. I have no doubt that it was brought on by the stress I have been under.

When I was admitted, I knew that Mother was in a bed just a few doors away. She had been hospitalized four days earlier for treatment of back pain. I thought of picking up the telephone and asking the switchboard operator to connect me with Mother's room, but I felt so sick that I decided I would wait a day or two. I shouldn't have. Mother died the following afternoon.

When Dad came into my room to tell me, I was certain I had fallen into a deep sleep and was having a nightmare. It wouldn't be unusual to dream of death after losing Tom, I thought.

But no, it was real. A doctor was standing at the foot of my bed saying, "We're not sure what happened. It had

43

nothing to do with the back pain. It looks as though your mother coughed hard and somehow ruptured her esophagus. She died within minutes."

Even with medication, it was hours before I could get to sleep that night. A nurse came in and sat with me for a few minutes. "Why can't I cry?" I asked.

"You've lost too much too soon," she explained. "First your husband, now your mother. Your mind can't take it all in. Be patient with yourself."

I keep remembering how Mother said "I love you" just a few weeks ago. I'm glad she gave me that special gift. It makes the loss easier to bear, as do her age and the swiftness of her death. At seventy-nine she had lived a full life span and was active for most of it. When I think of how some of my friends have had to watch the slow, lingering deterioration of their mothers and fathers, I am grateful that I did not have to experience that kind of heartbreak.

JULY 6

While I was in the hospital, the nurses who took care of Tom in the intensive care unit were kind enough to stop by my room and visit briefly. They all told me how much they wanted Tom to live. I could only sob and say over and over again that Tom was the center of my life, half of me had been torn away, and I had never known such agony.

One nurse sat on the edge of my bed and held my hand. "Tom taught us a lot about life," she said. "We cried when he didn't pull through. We feel his loss, too, Bev. It isn't just yours."

I felt ashamed. I was guilty of being self-centered about Tom's death. Of course nobody could feel his loss as

44

deeply as I, but I had lost sight of how much his death has affected others—his students, his co-workers, his friends, even the people who had nursed him through two heart attacks. I wondered how I could have been so blind.

It was the same with Tom's doctor. I told him I was angry with him because I thought he had given me false hope during Tom's last days. I even confessed that I had wondered if he and Tom had made a pact whereby they had agreed to give me nothing but optimistic reports of Tom's condition.

Dr. Forssell assured me that there was no truth to my line of thinking. He was sorry if his daily reports had misled me. Then he turned his head away, looked out the window, and added, "It is always difficult to lose a patient, and it was especially hard to lose Tom. He was young and had so much to give."

Again, I felt ashamed that my grief had made me so blind and insensitive.

JULY 7

I feel at war with myself. Part of me says I must let go of Tom; another resists the idea. I have decided, however, that if I am to have any sense of peace in my heart, I have to surrender. I must let him go.

While I was resting this afternoon, I pictured a balloon with Tom's face on it and a string trailing behind. I clenched my hand as if to hold the string, then deliberately opened it. The balloon floated away from me, higher and higher, until it was out of sight.

This does not mean forgetting Tom. That could never happen. He is close to me in spirit. He is in my memory and sometimes in my dreams at night. I wear his wedding ring next to mine as a symbol of my abiding love for him. The letting go simply means that I have accepted his death.

Ever since Tom died, it has been as if I were in a deep, dark pit marked GRIEF. Somewhere overhead there is light, and I want to reach it. The letting go today was like finding a toehold on the wall of the pit. I am starting to climb out.

II

As to how I take sorrow, the answer is, "In all the possible ways." Because, as you probably know, it isn't a state but a process. It keeps on changing—like a winding road with quite a new landscape at each bend.

—C. S. LEWIS

JULY 8

ELIZABETH CAME TO SEE ME this morning. I always enjoy a visit with her. While at seventy-six she is many years my senior, I never think of that when we are together. She carries herself straight and tall, moves with sureness, and has more zest for life than some of my younger friends. But what I like best about Elizabeth is the way she opens my mind to deeper thought. Sometimes it is through her own words of wisdom, other times it is through a suggestion of something to read—like today. She gave me a booklet, *God Works in Wondrous Ways*.

"You might want to read the section called 'When One Door Opens,'" Elizabeth said. "The words may speak to you."

They did, and I am beginning to see that there are no endings. Each ending is actually the beginning of something else.

A door marked LIFE WITH TOM has been closed against my will; slammed in my face. No key will unlock it. No amount of pounding will open it. No amount of kicking will knock it down. In agony I accept that, just as yesterday I accepted Tom's death. Surely if I look for another door I shall find it, and while it will not lead me to the same place or bring me the kind of happiness I once knew, at least it will take me out of the nowhere in which I find myself these days. And the door will open easily. All I need do is turn the knob and push gently.

But I must open the door myself, and I must believe that God will be on the other side to walk a new path with me—guiding, strengthening, giving purpose to my life. I have to ask Him for that, because I know I can't walk a new way without Him.

JULY 10

The emotional ups and downs of grief are draining. My outlook is positive one minute, negative the next. Sometimes I can't even find a reason for the mood swings, but today I know why I am at a low point.

I am in bed with an attack of vertigo, the MS symptom I hate most. That alone is enough to dampen my spirits, but there is more. Today is Tom's birthday.

As much as I am trying to keep my thoughts forward-looking, it is difficult not to look back when certain dates on the calendar come along. As soon as I woke up this morning I thought of birthdays past and the fun of them. It was all right at first, but then my spirits plummeted. "The rest of my life without Tom" is a phrase that has been running through my head all day. I am depressed and can't seem to do anything except cry and hug Tom's pillow.

48

To make matters worse, the cardinal that has sung to me every morning since Tom died has been silent for the past three days. I miss it. It symbolized Tom for me. I wonder if it is a coincidence that it stopped singing the day after I let go of Tom.

JULY 11

Elizabeth told me recently how she watched the eclipse of the moon a week or so ago. She wrapped herself in a blanket to keep warm and sat on her back steps. What impressed her was that in its fullness, the moon was such a large, bright, obvious light in the sky that only in the darkness of eclipse did she notice the smaller lights—the stars.

I have been thinking of this in a different way.

While the bright light in my life has gone out, I need not feel that I am in total darkness. There are smaller lights to guide my way. Like the stars Elizabeth spoke of, they have been there all the time, but my eyes were centered on the moon. They are my family and friends; and perhaps now even some new but as yet still-hidden purpose to my life.

If the moon were to be obscured behind a cloud forever, it would be missed, and the nights would never have the same brilliance as before; but the stars would be in the heavens, shining like millions of small candles and giving at least some measure of light. Life would go on, only with a change in what was familiar.

And so it is with me. My life will never be the same again, but it goes on. I have to adjust my vision to less light.

JULY 12

Some weeks ago, Debbie's young friend Barbara asked if she could plant seeds in the space where Tom had his vegetable garden. Of course I said yes. As with everything that was Tom's, I want it used, not enshrined.

This afternoon Barbara and two of her friends were here to pull weeds and to harvest the first beans. Their voices, their laughter, and their singing drifted across the backyard into an open window in my room. It was comforting, but I wasn't sure why. Later it came to me. Conversation, laughter, singing—they all add up to life. I have been so preoccupied with death that I had nearly forgotten the sounds of life.

Surely to overcome the sorrow of death there must be a touchstone with life. I think I was first aware of it when I sensed that I was drawing energy from the people who gave me their loving support in the immediate weeks after Tom died, but today the feeling grew.

I have been thinking of this concerning Tom's mother. I feel badly that she is alone and lives so far away that I cannot visit with her except by long-distance telephone calls. She sobs and keeps asking why Tom had to die. "All I do is sit and stare out the window or look at Tom's picture," she said one day. Again and again, I have asked if anyone comes to see her. The reply is always the same. "I don't want to see anyone. I want to be left alone."

I think Mom is wrong to shut herself away. She needs to share her grief, and she needs some touchstone with life. I am sure it would ease the ache in her heart, as it has in mine. I can't imagine trying to survive the torment of deep loss without the support of other people, and today I learned how vital it is to connect with life as well.

JULY 15

It seems impossible that my sorrow could be deeper at this point, and yet I find that it is. Perhaps shock had

50

numbed me and now it has worn off, and I am more aware of the wound.

There is a constant longing that reminds me of the homesickness I felt when I first went off to college, and of the lonely, lost feeling I had years later when Tom went to summer school halfway across the country and I stayed behind.

Nothing is in harmony. I have no appetite, and I wake up in the middle of the night crying. Most of all, I am preoccupied with every detail of Tom's last days. The memory of them simply will not leave me, especially his phone call just minutes before he died. I pound my fists and cry out to the walls that Tom said his good-by to me, but I didn't have a chance to say mine to him. I feel cheated. I needed to hold him close one last time and tell him how much happiness he gave me.

When I shared all of this with Connie, she said, "Was it really necessary to say good-by?"

I thought for a few minutes. "No, I suppose not."

In truth, it wouldn't have made any difference. Tom knew how deeply I loved him, and no matter how many hours I might have spent holding him close and talking to him, it would not have been enough. I would have wanted more and more time. Still, it is like unfinished business. Tom and I never parted without a kiss and hug, not even if he was just going to work or downtown for an errand. In spite of what I said to Connie, I am unhappy about not saying good-by to Tom the way I wanted to.

JULY 17

After I finished my physical therapy exercises in the swimming pool this afternoon, Connie and I splashed around in the water and all at once I heard myself laughing. I felt alive, full of joy, happy and intensely aware of everything around me—the warmth of the sun on my face and arms, the blue sky, the color of the water and the way it lapped against the sides of the pool when my movements stirred it up. It was as if something magical had happened and at the snap of a finger I had become my old self again.

Oddly enough, however, I had at the same time a sense of guilt. Tom was dead. I had no right to feel such joy.

I thought about it later. To feel guilty over being happy would be to punish myself for no reason. I won't do it. I have accepted Tom's death, and I am starting to climb out of the dark pit of grief. Self-punishment would do nothing except knock me to the bottom again. I needed the magic moment that captured me this afternoon. It is a ray of hope that eventually I am going to be all right and that my life did not end with Tom's.

July 19

Debbie has been dating a young man, and I told her she could bring him here for dinner last night. I had no idea what an emotional impact it would have on me.

A deep longing gripped me when I saw Debbie and her friend together. Their hand holding and their affectionate glances pierced my heart, stirring up memories and painfully reminding me of what I have lost. I am not proud of the envy I felt, but it was there.

I told Mary about it. "Being envious of couples is not unusual for a widow," she said. "Sometimes it hits me in church when I see husbands and wives sitting together. It hurts. I feel left out."

There is so much to overcome as a widow—anger, bitterness, loneliness, fear, depression, self-pity, guilt, envy. No wonder it is such a devastating experience.

I don't know how to handle all the bewildering emotions except to take them as they come and learn from them. Honesty and rationalization both help. If I can face the emotion straight on and analyze why it takes hold of me, I think I can conquer it.

I may never again feel envy as deeply as I did last night. Today I realize how foolish it was. Some women go through life without ever knowing the kind of love I have known. It was a precious gift, and though it is gone now, except as a memory, at least I had it once. There is no reason for me to feel envious.

JULY 22

I was in my room writing a letter this morning when I heard a bird in the cranberry bush just outside my window. I was so engrossed in what I was doing, however, that I didn't want to take time for bird-watching. But the "tit, tit" sound continued, and finally curiosity got the better of me, and I wheeled myself to the window.

My heart jumped. There, sitting on a branch and peering directly into my room, was a cardinal. Tears filled my eyes as I stared at the beautiful creature. He stayed for a minute or two, then flew off into a tree, where he sang his song before disappearing.

I was elated and sad at the same time. Could the cardinal be Tom's spirit coming to say hello? I wondered. Whether or not such a thing is possible doesn't matter. My heart tells me that Tom is close by today.

Later this afternoon the autopsy report on Tom arrived

in the mail. Most of it is medical jargon—aneurysm, myocardial infarction, mural thrombi, pulmonary edema, absent left circumflex coronary artery (apparently a birth defect). I spent an hour with the report in one hand and the dictionary in the other. It is clear that Tom did not stand a chance in a million. There was no way he could have survived the massive damage to his body.

Seeing everything in writing puts a lot of questions to rest. I know that Tom received proper care and that nothing could have saved his life. In truth, I was lucky to have him as long as I did. I know, too, that while losing him so suddenly seems unjust, it was for the best. If he had lived, he would have suffered pain, frustration, and unhappiness. I wouldn't want that for Tom. I loved him too much.

July 26

A few weeks ago I decided to sell the double bed in which Tom and I slept for all the years of our marriage. Reaching out to that empty space beside me night after night had become more than I could bear. Yesterday the old bed went to a secondhand furniture shop, and a twin-size bed arrived and was set up in my room.

I cried before I went to sleep last night. The new bed was a sharp reminder of the singleness of my life, and I wondered if I had been right in buying it. Memories came in a rush. I thought of all the warm, secure closeness I had known next to Tom in our bed, the tender lovemaking, the snuggling up on cold winter nights. I thought of how we sometimes lay quietly in the dark, holding hands and talking.

It hurts to acknowledge that all of that is gone, and yet I

must. Perhaps the fact that I found the courage to part with something as intimate and personally meaningful as the double bed is a sign that I am moving forward in my life, even though most of the time I feel as if I am standing still.

AUGUST 1

The worst part of being a widow is the loneliness, I think. It is like a disease eating away at the insides—a slow, torturous gnawing, an unrelenting ache. When you have shared your life with someone, there is a cavernous gap after your partner is gone.

I miss Tom in so many ways. It doesn't seem right to wake up in the morning or to go to sleep at night without him beside me, or to move through the days without his companionship.

It helps to have Debbie and my friends coming and going and to be busy with paperwork and running the house, but nothing closes the gap completely. And no matter how full my day may be, there is always that moment when I turn out the light at bedtime and come face to face with my loneliness. I am filled with it until merciful sleep overtakes me.

Weekends are no easier now than they were at the start. A dread of them begins to take hold of me as early as Thursday night. Connie found me in tears one Sunday recently. "It's the weekend," I sobbed.

"Did you and Tom used to do something special on weekends?" Connie asked.

"No, nothing special. It's just that we were together."

I'm not sure that Connie understood, but I could not explain it any more clearly.

Certain specific hours on weekdays are as difficult as *every* hour of the weekends. Four o'clock is my low point. Tom's car should be pulling into the driveway, and he should be coming through the door to kiss me hello. Even if I'm not looking at the clock, I have a sense of what time it is. A sudden wave of loneliness comes over me. The supper hour brings another emotional dip. I should be setting a place for Tom at the table. He should be there to eat with me, to tell me about his day, and to listen to the events of mine.

While I can remember other times of loneliness in my life, what I am experiencing now as a widow must be the ultimate.

The only way I know how to make lonely hours fly is to write, so my pen and a pad of yellow-lined paper are always at hand these days. I feel ready for it and am writing some poems for children. It is good to be working creatively again after what seems so long away from it.

AUGUST 6

The funeral director called to say that the marker for Tom's grave is in place, so Connie took me to see it. Having something more to look at than a plot of grass made it less painful to be at the grave, but I still cried. The wound in my heart is far from healed.

Tom has been gone nearly four months. I long to know where he is and what he is doing. It is as if he were on a trip and has not written or telephoned to share it with me.

AUGUST 9

While I feel totally separated from Tom and have yet to experience a strong sense of his "presence," there is still reason for me to believe that he is near.

Several times it has come to me that I should take care of certain matters. It usually happens within seconds of waking up in the morning. Today something told me to check the level of filter material that is part of the water-softening system in the house. Since it only needs attention every two years, is in the basement out of my sight, and was never my responsibility, there was really nothing to remind me of it. I decided to have the plumber look at it.

"It's a good thing you called," he said after coming upstairs from the basement. "You were about an inch away from being out of that filtering material."

Surely I am being guided and watched over.

AUGUST 12

For weeks now, I have been making phone calls, writing letters, and talking to people in an effort to replace Debbie. She is leaving on the sixteenth.

I have had no luck and am in such despair that I'm seriously thinking of not staying in this house. How can I, when MS does not allow me to be independent?

All possible leads turn out to be impossible. So far, I have interviewed two people who spent most of the time telling me how desperately lonely they are, even to the point of wanting to commit suicide. My first thought was that if they felt needed, it might ease their depression, and therefore I should consider them carefully and choose the one who would suit me best. I took their telephone numbers and said I would be in touch in a day or two.

I gave it some thought and decided it would be better to find someone who is not depressed. It is hard enough to deal with my own emotions.

Yesterday a young woman telephoned to say she heard I was looking for someone to live in and could she come and talk. She arrived with a friend, and it soon became apparent that what they had in mind was a "package deal." They are presently roommates and do not want to separate. I explained that there was only one extra room and it was too small for two people. "I could sleep on the floor in a sleeping bag," one of them said.

It was difficult to discourage those girls, but I had to. When we said good-by, they promised to stop in from time to time to see how I am doing. Whether or not I'll ever see them again doesn't matter. Their youthful enthusiasm, their caring, were in refreshing contrast to the depressed, self-centered women I talked to last week.

AUGUST 17

Debbie moved out yesterday. She went to Maine for a week's vacation with her family before starting nursing school. We were both sad.

Ever since Tom died, I find it difficult to say good-by to people, so I asked Debbie to just walk out the door as if she were going to work. But she couldn't do it. As soon as her car was packed, she came into my room, gave me a quick hug, and thanked me for having her here.

The search for someone to replace Debbie goes on. Meanwhile, I have worked things out as best I can. I have hired a girl to cook suppers, and Connie insists on spending the nights with me, coming in during the evening at her convenience and sleeping in Debbie's room.

All the kindness that has come to me these past few months is heartwarming, and I wish I knew how to repay it. Connie says I already have, simply by allowing others to help me. "You are giving people more joy than you realize," she explained.

AUGUST 19

Today is our wedding anniversary. I woke thinking of the happiness I felt fifteen years ago. In my mind I went back to that time—the exchange of vows at the church parsonage, the camping honeymoon in a tent that leaked when it rained, the wondrous joy of being together every minute of the day and night.

I cried for a little while this morning, but did not allow myself to be blue all day. My life with Tom was wonderful in every way, and the memories are sweet.

When Connie came in this evening, she was holding two roses in a vase. "These are for you," she said. "They are from Tom for your anniversary. The moment I found them in my rose garden I knew why they were there."

I smiled. The roses really did seem as if they were from Tom. He often surprised me in such a way on our anniversary.

AUGUST 23

I have just finished reading Raymond Moody's *Life After Life*, case histories of people who revealed what happened to them when they were declared "clinically dead" and subsequently revived. Their descriptions of the death experience were totally engrossing, giving me a sense of what Tom may have gone through when he died.

Death is nothing to fear. Life on "the other side" is beautiful, peaceful, filled with light, I am convinced. I firmly believe that Tom has simply passed from life as we know it here on earth to life in a different place, on a different plane of existence. He is happy. His grandparents, father, and two sisters who made the transition before him were there with a welcome.

And I have no doubt that I will be with Tom again someday. While the time between now and then will seem long for me, for him it will be as if we had been separated for only a brief moment.

I wonder how anyone can get through the sorrow of death without a belief in life hereafter. It is comforting to know that there will be a reunion. The good-by is not final.

AUGUST 30

When Ferris visited Tom in the hospital one day, he told her, "I'm not afraid to die. I'm only afraid of the mess I will leave Bev in."

At this point, that's how I feel—in a mess. I still have not found a replacement for Debbie. I have contacted every source I can think of—the rehabilitation center where Debbie worked, four colleges in the area, the superintendent of schools in case there may be a teacher looking for housing, ministers, and all likely human service agencies listed in the telephone book. I have also placed an ad in the newspaper.

So far, no luck. My life seems uncertain. Tom was my anchor; I am drifting in circles, going nowhere.

SEPTEMBER 2

It seems best to let the tears fall rather than to hold them back. More often than not it is some small, unexpected thing that brings them to the surface.

When I saw a school bus pass the house yesterday, a

surge of loneliness swept over me, and I cried. It doesn't seem right that Tom is not here to be part of the new school year. I thought of his desk and chair in the science room at school and pictured them empty, even though I know they are not.

Last night Connie and I talked for a while about loss and grief. "How would you define grieving?" she asked. I couldn't answer her then, but I have given it some thought today, and this is my definition: Grieving is the painful, heart-wrenching process of adjusting to a shattering event that has taken away something that was dear, meaningful, and familiar.

SEPTEMBER 6

Today's mail brought *Story Friends*, the children's magazine in which a poem I sold last year has been published. When I told Connie how much I wish Tom could know of it, she said, "But he does know."

Seeing my words in print lifted my spirits higher than they have been in months and is an incentive to do more writing, study markets for my work, and start sending things out to publishers.

SEPTEMBER 10

I am beginning to get some response from the ad I placed in the newspaper and from other sources as well. I have been interviewing a variety of women all week.

One was an eighty-year-old vegetarian who is a member of some far-out religious group; she wanted a place to live for only three weeks, and added, "Of course you'll keep your home health aide. I'm no good at taking care of people."

Another was also a vegetarian, but young and at least willing to give me the help I need. I asked her if she could cook. "I know how to fix hot dogs and fish," she said. Curious cooking skills for a vegetarian! All the same, I was tempted to give her serious consideration (perhaps I could broaden her cooking skills), but changed my mind when she insisted on keeping two cats in her bedroom.

Some leads did not reach the interview stage. An amusing call came from the dean of women at one of the colleges nearby. "Would you take a man professor?" she asked. I said no and reminded her that I need help taking a shower and getting dressed. When I laughed and she didn't, I wondered about her age and whether I might be on the older side of a generation gap.

A social worker from one of the human service agencies called to inquire if I would consider taking a mother with a nine-year old son. When I explained that there was only one small extra room, the social worker said, "We don't care." But I do.

SEPTEMBER 11

A letter from Jane today brought the news that she is divorcing her husband. As a long-time friend, I should answer Jane in a sympathetic, supportive way, but I can't find the right words. She is deliberately putting her husband out of her life; mine is gone against my will, and I would give anything to have him back.

The days ahead will be a kind of grieving period for Jane, and in the end, there may be more anguish for her as a divorcée than there is for me as a widow. Because there is to be joint custody of the children, Jane will continue to have some contact with the man she once loved. He may even marry again. Divorce does not have the finality of death.

SEPTEMBER 15

I am beginning to wonder if I should have placed that ad in the newspaper. It draws the most unlikely candidates.

Yesterday an unemployed eighteen-year-old girl telephoned. I explained that she would need a job because I am not offering a salary, only free room and board. "What job skills do you have?" I asked.

"I know how to pick apples," was the answer. I didn't bother to set up an interview.

But by far the saddest response to my ad came this afternoon. A woman called to ask if she could see me at once. She arrived with her husband, who sat on one side of the room, silent, head down, nervously tapping his foot. She sat on the other side, throwing poisonous glances in his direction. Finally she began to cry. "He's divorcing me," she said. "I'm sixty-five years old, have just had cancer surgery, and can't manage the house alone. I might as well give up everything and live somewhere else, or commit suicide."

The woman wouldn't stop talking. Even when I finally said I didn't think this was the right situation for her, it was an hour before she and her husband got up and left.

My own troubles seem nothing compared to what I heard today.

SEPTEMBER 16

Mary has an idea. A girl she had as a student in special needs class graduated in June and now wants to take a first step away from home. Mary thinks Tina would be the

63

perfect replacement for Debbie and that the girl would grow in many ways from the experience of being with me.

I have talked with a guidance counselor at school who knows Tina well and is helping her find a job and a place to live. He likes the idea and has arranged for me to meet her tomorrow.

SEPTEMBER 17

I think I am nearing the end of my long search. The meeting-interview went well today. Tina is an attractive twenty-year-old with clear, fair skin, deep blue eyes, and a shy manner. She kept her head down and played nervously with her long brown hair while we talked.

I have agreed to get in touch with her in a few days. Mostly it is to give her some time to think things over. As for me, I have already made up my mind.

Everything about Tina seems right. She expects to start a part-time job soon and impressed me as a capable, responsible girl. And there is more. The school wants me to teach her basic living skills such as cooking, shopping, housekeeping, and budgeting. I would love to be a teacher again, even if not in the way I once knew.

I have been wondering how Tom would feel about all of this. I believe he would see it not only as a teaching challenge for me, but as an opportunity to help a young person get started in life, so it seems doubly right.

SEPTEMBER 23

Tina decided to accept my offer. She walked in last night with her clothes in cardboard boxes and a stuffed animal under her arm. I went to bed thinking of what a long road it was to finding her and how God answers prayers in His own way and in His own time.

OCTOBER 6

Today my thoughts turned to the period when Tom was recovering from his first heart attack. Fear of widowhood was real. It anchored itself in a corner of my mind, staying with me every moment of the day and sometimes keeping me awake for hours in the middle of the night. The thoughts went unspoken, but Tom knew they were there. "I think we had better have a 'what if' talk," he said one evening.

I only half-listened when he told me where I would find his insurance policies and other important papers. Weeping, I declared, "If you should die, I would die, too."

"No, you wouldn't," Tom said. "I know you would have the courage to go on alone. I want you to remember that."

I don't know why that conversation came back to me today, but I am glad it did. It's been a day of feeling depressed, and Tom's words give me something to hold on to.

I suppose most married couples who are deeply in love feel that if death should separate them, life would be unbearable for the survivor. But the fact is that life does go on for the one who is left. And statistics show that the chances of a wife outliving her husband are greater than the other way around. I knew that, but I always thought it would happen to someone else, not me.

III

It isn't for the moment you are struck that you need courage, but for the long uphill climb back to sanity and faith and security.

—ANNE MORROW LINDBERGH

OCTOBER 9

TODAY MARKS THE MIDPOINT of this first year alone, and it seems a proper time for assessing where I stand.

I think the worst is behind me. Even though I plummet now and then, I have learned that it is only a temporary falling back. Somehow I pick myself up and start over.

I still feel the deep, agonizing pain of grief, but I have let go of Tom, and that was an important step. There is no more pounding of fists or screaming at the walls in rebellion of what has happened, and I've stopped asking why it had to happen. I have accepted that there is no answer, just as I have accepted Tom's death.

On the practical side, things have smoothed out. The business of settling Tom's estate is moving along, my finances are in order, Tina is here and handles her responsibilities well. I've been moving forward, not standing still, even though at times it seems at a slow pace.

Loneliness is the biggest problem. It gnaws at me. While

the daytime hours are filled with writing and the busyness of running the house, and in the evenings I escape lonely silence through reading or watching television, sometimes I think I can't stand another minute without Tom. He is close to me in a spiritual way all the time now, but that doesn't take the place of his physical presence. I need to be gathered in his arms and to hear his voice saying, "I love you, Hon."

I have passed two milestones — Tom's birthday and our wedding anniversary. They brought tears and sorrow upon sorrow, and yet I survived them. The months ahead hold two big holidays and my birthday, but I am trying not to think about that. More and more, I am learning how to live only one day at a time.

OCTOBER 17

Roland has been cleaning the basement. (What would I do without good friends?) I asked him to keep an eye out for two old shoeboxes tied with ribbon. He found them yesterday. They are filled with letters from Tom and mine to him, written the year before we were married. I stayed up late last night reading some of them.

Seeing Tom's handwriting and reading his words to me brought him close. It was wonderful. I went to bed feeling happy.

I spent most of today with the letters, too. I couldn't resist them. They took me back to a time that was wondrous. But suddenly this afternoon I could not bear to read another word. It was too painful a reminder of the tender love, understanding, and companionship I have lost. I cried long and hard and have packed the letters away in a drawer.

October 21

"The first thing a child should learn is how to endure. It is what he will have most need to know."

When I came across these words by Jean-Jacques Rousseau today, I thought of how wise they are and how, as a widow, I am facing the supreme test of endurance. I wonder if I can live day after day, year after year, without the person who gave meaning to my life.

I can only hope that as a child, or somewhere along the way, I have learned "how to endure," for surely there is no one who can teach me such a hard lesson.

Connie says I should keep telling myself that everything will be all right. God has a plan for me, and I must be open to His direction. But it is all so difficult.

October 27

Running the house is easier now that Tina is here, but there are still times when I wish I didn't have the responsibility of it. I have to depend on others too much — someone to drive Tina to the grocery store, someone else to do post office and general errands, another to take the trash to the dump.

I was dependent on Tom for many things, too, but that was different. Sharing the load was simply part of being marriage partners. Now I feel like a nuisance. And there is a fear that sooner or later, the supportive people who bring order to my day-to-day living will not be there for me. It is a fear born out of losing Tom, and though I do not like to think of it, I must remember that nothing is forever, change is inevitable. The comfortable rhythm of my life could easily be interrupted all too abruptly again.

Wondering how my experience compares with that of others, I have been reading books on widowhood. What it comes down to is that while there are three classic stages of grief (generally called shock, suffering, and recovery), the grieving process itself and the time it takes to move from one stage to another is an individual and personal matter. Much depends on age, personality, and above all, what kind of marriage the couple had.

To be widowed at any age would not be easy for me, but losing Tom in the productive years of his life somehow makes it seem worse. He was denied a full life span; I have been left with too many years to carry on alone.

One day when I looked at Tom's most recent photograph I realized that I'll grow older and my looks will change, but I shall always remember Tom just as he is in that picture. I'll never know what he would have looked like as an old man, any more than I'll know what the years of retirement would have been like for us.

I wonder what gives one widow more personal courage than another. Perhaps it has to do with a strong faith in God; perhaps the lessons of grief were learned through some earlier traumatic loss; perhaps intelligence makes the difference. If a widow can grasp the reality of her loss intellectually and try to understand the why of every emotion she experiences in her new state, she may come to terms with her sorrow more easily than someone who attempts to avoid the pain through alcohol, drugs, or sexual escapades.

I haven't any measure of my own courage. I know I've been up and I've been down and I have handled the emotional roller-coaster rides in various ways. Sometimes prayer has carried me, sometimes the support of friends has held me together, and sometimes it has been my own digging down into a well of determination to overcome loss.

The kind of marriage I had is what makes widowhood so devastating to me. Tom and I were happy. He was the center of my life; I was the center of his. It is that simple. I have lost half of myself.

NOVEMBER 10

I am depressed and have not been sleeping or eating well lately. I wake up in the middle of the night and seldom get back to sleep. I lie in the darkness, thinking. At mealtime my stomach feels nervous, and I pick at my food. It was the same in the immediate weeks after Tom died. What has pushed me back?

Perhaps it is that my little corner of New Hampshire is in a period of dark, gloomy November weather after a golden autumn, and I am aware that my first winter without Tom will soon be here. Mary says the first of everything is difficult for a widow, including a change of seasons.

Or maybe I am depressed because I have been reading Tom's letters again. I feel drawn to them and to some of my old journals, as well. I know I should not cling to the past, but the need to connect with Tom is very strong these days, and the letters and journals help. While I am pulled down emotionally afterward, at least for the few hours that the letters and journals take me back to another time and place the pain of loneliness is anesthetized.

NOVEMBER 15

Utter despair came over me like a sudden storm cloud this morning. I was reminded of something Mary once told me. Several months after Russell died, there was a day when she felt totally desperate with loneliness and sorrow. She was at her lowest point emotionally. Then all at once she reached out with her hands and said, "I trust You, Lord." She put herself in God's care and within moments felt a new confidence, a firm belief that everything was going to be all right.

If I did not actually hit my lowest emotional point this morning, I came as close to it as I ever want to. And while I did not reach out to God with my hands, as Mary did, or experience the carefree trust that captured her, at least I prayed and felt better.

I don't know how anyone can work through grief without a measure of faith in God. Mine is not as strong as Mary's, but it is growing. When I asked for courage today, it came. The storm cloud passed, and I dried my tears.

I sometimes wonder why I am so slow to remember that God is there for me, and that all I need do is ask for His help and guidance.

NOVEMBER 19

The television Christmas blitz has started. At times I feel like pulling the plug on the set until January. Every ad centers on romantic couples and happy family gatherings. It brings to mind how different the holidays will be for me this year. Tom is gone, Mother is gone.

I have made up my mind not to accept any Thanksgiving or Christmas Day invitations. I know there are those who will press me to change my mind, but I shall have to make them understand that I need to trust my own feelings on matters like this, to listen to my inner self, and to be assertive about what I think is best for me. I would rather stay home in familiar, comfortable surroundings this year, so when I discovered that Mary would be alone on Thanksgiving Day and that Debbie is not going home for Christmas, I invited them to share those holidays with me.

NOVEMBER 25. THANKSGIVING

I was awake earlier than usual this morning and said an immediate thanks for the sun after a nine-day period of gloomy weather. Tears came with the thought of last year's Thanksgiving—just Tom and me having a quiet dinner at home, grateful that he was recovering nicely from the July heart attack. I ached with wanting him to be here today, wanting things to be as they once were.

Tina went home after breakfast, and I was alone until Mary came in the early afternoon with a beef stew she had made. We ate our nontraditional Thanksgiving dinner on trays in the living room where we could sit in the warmth of the sunlight and enjoy the view from the big window. "I love to sit here and look out at the mountains," Mary said. "It's so peaceful."

I thought of the psalm that was read at Tom's memorial service—"I will lift up mine eyes unto the hills; from whence cometh my help?"

And so I have passed another milestone.

NOVEMBER 30

I have noticed a change in the behavior of two women friends whose marriages are still intact. When either of them stops by in the company of her husband, she clings to his arm, holds his hand, or gazes adoringly at him.

If this were the usual behavior of these women I wouldn't give it a second thought, but it strikes me as suddenly different and has me wondering. Does being with me remind these women that they too could be widowed one day? Do they therefore want more than ever to display an appreciation of their mates? Or is it that I am seen as a threat to the marriage?

Mary says she had the same experience. Several of her married women friends behaved coldly toward her after Russell died, and some made no effort to maintain a friendship as before.

I do not consider myself a threat. I have absolutely no interest in anyone else's husband, nor does any husband have an interest in me.

DECEMBER 6

While cleaning out a closet today, I came across a large manila envelope containing letters Tom sent to me when I was hospitalized at various times during our married years. He would visit me every day, but he wrote daily letters, too. They are filled with love, concern, and expressions of loneliness. It brought to mind the one letter I wrote to Tom when he was in the hospital last April. It was to tell him how much I loved him, missed him, wanted him to get well. The day after he died, the letter was in my mailbox marked "Return to Sender." It did not reach Tom in time.

I feel guilty. I should have written more than one letter, and sooner. And I should have spent more hours at Tom's bedside. I let him down. I wish I had ignored his pleas to save my strength, and I wish I hadn't been so naïve as to believe optimistic reports on his condition. If I had known how little time was left, nothing would have kept me from being with Tom.

I keep telling myself that it is foolish to carry guilt on top of sorrow, but it is there, nonetheless, and I don't know how to get rid of it.

DECEMBER 10

When I mail-ordered presents for Tina and Debbie today, I silently thanked them for giving me a reason to even think of Christmas this year. It made me realize, too, how much I like having young people in my life. They symbolize hope and the future in these days when I am more drawn to living one day at a time.

Debbie comes by now and then to share with me the ups and downs of nursing school. Her visits are a bright reminder that in spite of what has happened, the world is still turning.

It is the same with Tina, only on a daily basis. She is not ready to be on her own as far as cooking is concerned, so after breakfast we discuss what we'll have for supper and how much of it can be fixed ahead of time with my help. I am forced to think, plan, and be part of the world through the business of day-to-day living.

DECEMBER 15

Connie recently went to a "Laughter and Healing" seminar where one of the speakers was Norman Cousins, author of *Anatomy of an Illness*. Connie says Cousins believes that there may be some truth to the idea of choosing a time to die. A person's will to die is sometimes stronger than the will to live.

As I think of Tom's last days, I wonder if he gave up when he was told that he had suffered a second massive heart attack. After the first one, he was full of anger at what his body had done to him. When he was recovering and had to live with restrictions and limitations, he once said, "I might as well be dead. Now there are two of us who need to be taken care of."

Again, I feel guilty about not spending more time with Tom at the hospital. I could have assured him that everything would be all right, we would work it out.

I keep asking myself if it would have made any difference. Part of me says yes; and yet I know what the autopsy report showed. It was a miracle that Tom lived as long as he did.

It will be a while before I put my thoughts to rest on the matter. Guilt clouds logic.

DECEMBER 20

I am so depressed about Christmas that Connie suggested we read something to help focus on the real meaning of the holiday. I chose Elizabeth Yates' book *On That Night*. Elizabeth's visits and the long talks we have had these past months have deepened our friendship and made me want more than ever to read her books.

Yesterday Connie began reading the book aloud to me. Its theme is that on Christmas Eve, things lost are found again. There is a young widow in the story whose loneliness and grief I readily understand. Speaking of her late husband, she says to a stranger (in truth, Christ) who walks with her after a Christmas Eve candlelight service, "I needed him so much, and he needed me; and life was bliss . . . Life without him looks very long, and bleak, and dark."

The Stranger then leads the widow to realize that "what she had lost she would pine for no longer; instead, she would live what had been richly given her and so doing affirm life."

I was so deeply moved by these words that I wept. "Perhaps you were meant to read this book," Connie said.

I thought about it the rest of the day and through a restless sleep last night.

Tom gave me love, taught me the purest meaning of devotion and caring, made me happy. But now, like the widow in the story, I must stop pining. I must affirm life. I'm not sure how to do it except to begin by reminding myself every day that love is what matters most, that I should look for opportunities to give it abundantly, and that through love my life will take on a new meaning.

December 26

"Try to think of it as just another day," Mary said when I expressed a dread of my first Christmas without Tom. I remembered her advice several times yesterday when moments of intense loneliness came in sudden waves, and it helped.

Debbie cooked a wonderful dinner, and Dad was here to share it with us, but it was the quietest holiday I have ever known and by far the saddest and least festive.

I considered having a Christmas tree, then changed my mind. I couldn't bear to unwrap the ornaments Tom and I had collected over the years. Instead, I settled for putting the little hand-carved wooden tree and a china angel on the kitchen table. Mostly it was for Tina, who a few days before Christmas asked if I was going to have any decorations around the house.

All my friends helped me get through the holiday with cards, letters, and telephone calls saying, "We are thinking of you." Mary did something special by dropping in unexpectedly Christmas Eve. I know it was her way of saying, "I remember the pain and loneliness of the first Christmas Eve as a widow."

So the biggest holiday of the year is over, and I am relieved to have it behind me. I survived it without going to pieces, and that's a victory, but not one I gained alone. I couldn't have done it without the loving support that came from all directions. The spirit of Christmas was truly evident. Gifts were in abundance; not in packages, but in acts of thoughtfulness, love, and caring, and that is what counts.

JANUARY 1. NEW YEAR'S DAY

How happy Tom and I were a year ago! There was so much to look forward to. Tom was making a remarkable recovery from his first heart attack, and our lives were returning to some degree of normality. We welcomed January first with a certainty that everything good was ahead for us.

But it wasn't, and as I approach the New Year without Tom, it seems a time to assess once again where I am in this grieving process.

Without any true awareness of it, I seem to have moved out of the suffering stage. I cry less often and feelings of deep longing are fleeting now instead of constant. Looking back, the suffering stage was more agonizing than the earlier period of shock, when there was numbness to insulate against the pain. And it lasted for a longer time. It was like a slow-burning candle that simply grew smaller and smaller until it finally sputtered out.

And now, if I am to move through the classic stages of grief, I must look next to recovery. Clearly there is a choice at this point. I can shut out the world by pulling the covers up over my head and dwelling on yesterdays and what used to be, or I can affirm life and feed its growth with renewed purpose, faith in God, and faith in myself.

I choose affirmation, even when I know it means facing a challenge again and again, making mistakes along the way, and falling back temporarily in defeat from time to time. It is a more difficult choice than shutting out the world, but my heart tells me it is the right one.

I remember a poster in the hallway of a rehabilitation center where I once went for physical therapy. It said, "Life is God's gift to you. What you do with it is your gift to God."

I believe those words, and no matter how deep my sorrow may be, it does not give me license to waste the rest of my life. I can't change what has happened, but I can control how much it will affect me, and I must remind myself of that every day of the new year ahead.

JANUARY 3. MY BIRTHDAY

Months ago when I thought of all the special occasions that would be sadly different without Tom, my birthday was the one that filled me with the most apprehension. I knew how much I would miss the carefully chosen card and present from Tom, the dinner cooked by him, and his voice saying, "I'm so glad you were born, Hon."

My heart ached when I opened my eyes this morning. I

78

asked God to give me an extra measure of courage to get through the day. What He granted was an outpouring of love from family and friends, and from that came courage. I cannot remember a birthday with as many cards, letters, and presents as this year. I feel happy and richly blessed with the greatest of all gifts — love.

JANUARY 8

Tina and I tidied up the house today, and it is now clear of any reminders of the holiday, except for Christmas cards, which I have been rereading.

I am deeply touched by the tender personal messages friends added to their cards. Marie wrote a long letter, and it brought such meaning that I want to record part of it in this journal:

A year ago, I was grieving the loss of my mother, and the holiday season held no joy for me. People told me that the first Christmas without her would be the hardest and that I would feel differently in the future, but I didn't believe them. I was sure the Christmas spirit had left me forever. This year, however, I have been surprised to find it filling me again.

While I know your loss is double because both your mother and Tom are gone, I still think I have a sense of how you must be feeling these days, and that is why I wanted to share with you what I experienced.

I don't know how I'll feel about Christmas in the future, but I am glad Marie told me what happened to her. It gives hope that I won't always dread the holiday season or have to think of Christmas as just another day. Perhaps next year Christmas joy will return to me as it did to Marie.

JANUARY 14

Today, after I copied down a new recipe in the notebook Tina and I have designated as her cookbook, I leafed through the pages and became aware of not only how many things Tina can now cook, but also of the part she plays in my battle with grief.

When I lost Tom, I lost my reason for being. Nobody was closely tied to my life anymore. But with Tina here, all of that has changed. In my role as head of household and "teacher," I have a responsibility to fulfill, an identity, a purpose. I feel needed.

And beyond that, Tina has awakened me to two joys I thought I would never know again—music and laughter.

After Tom died, I couldn't listen to music without crying, so I finally decided I would not turn on the radio except for morning news. Thanks to Tina, however, I have gradually overcome that. She often plays her radio and sings along with the tunes in her fine singing voice, and I cannot help overhearing it. Her musical taste is not mine, but I tolerate the pop music in small doses and find that I can even recognize one or two hit songs these days. In the end it all evens out. At breakfast, *my* radio is the one that is playing, and Tina's ears have to adapt to my preference for either classical or soft music.

As for laughter, Tina has a great sense of humor that especially comes to the surface when we watch something funny on television. Her laughter is infectious. I find myself going from a smile, to a chuckle, to a full-blown, hearty laugh. How good it feels!

JANUARY 16

We have been blessed with an unusually mild and snowless winter, until now. Snow began to fall yesterday and by last night a nor'easter was at full force. I worried. Would the strong winds leave us without electric power and, consequently, with no lights, heat, cooking facilities, or even water, since the well pump is also electric? Once Tom's worries, now they were mine—and with an added one. Last November I arranged to have a man plow the driveway. Would he remember to come?

Trusting in God is an ongoing test for me. I failed it when I worried and nearly failed it again this morning when I looked out to some ten inches of snow. A sense of hopelessness overcame me, and I shut the door to my room and cried.

What was troubling me, I decided, was not so much the snowstorm itself, but that the anxieties it brought were reminders of Tom's absence and my aloneness.

"O God, I'm not used to so much responsibility," I said out loud. I was startled. "O God," I had said. I was talking to Him, not to myself—the very thing I should have done purposely, not accidentally.

I stopped crying, said a prayer for courage, then had Tina open the back door so that I could wheel up to it and assess the situation. The driveway had been plowed. It wasn't the neat, precise job Tom would have done, but at least cars could get in and out. As for the steps and a path, I gave Tina brief instructions on how to shovel (she had never done it before) and off she went.

Again, I find that the first of everything as a widow is difficult. But as I meet each challenge, no matter how clumsily, lessons are learned. I am growing.

IV

A new heart I will give you, and a new spirit I will put within you.

—EZEKIEL 36:26

JANUARY 21

GRIEF IS CRUEL. It doesn't strike in one swift blow, then disappear. Aftershocks and sneak attacks are disguised in small things that are reminders of what used to be and will never be again. I give in to crying at such times, for I have come to think of my tears as a kind of baptism into the new life I am building. Besides, I know they will only be a brief shower, and soon I'll feel all right again.

This week the "small thing" is seed catalogues. The mail has been heavy with them, and they bring a pang. Tom is not here to plan ahead for his garden in the spring.

I can't stand to have the catalogues within my sight, so as soon as they arrive I put them in the pile of papers awaiting the next trip to the recycling center.

There is a cleansing aspect to getting rid of certain things that bring pain. I can hold them in my hand and actually toss them into a trash can, a fire, or the dump pile. It is a "letting go" in the literal sense.

None of this means that I am trying to forget Tom. It is,

rather, that as I walk this journey through grief, every time something gets in the way (even a small something) I am afraid I might stumble and fall if I do not remove it from my path. More than that, however, is the fact that memories lie in the heart, not in tangible objects, and my heart is filled with images of Tom. His face, his voice, his laugh and manner are as vivid to me as the sunshine that is streaming through the window at this very moment.

JANUARY 23

"According to Christian tradition, bells are an echo of the voice of God."

These words by Father Vincent Gallo refer to church bells, but when I read them today, I thought of them in a different light.

My doorbell and telephone echo the voice of God. Often when I am feeling lonely, someone comes to call or telephones unexpectedly. It is uncanny, even now when an earlier wide circle of friends has narrowed. Surely God is watching over me and knows when I need the comfort of another human being.

Just before I drop off to sleep at night, I say a prayer of thanks for the people who have touched my life in a loving, caring way during the course of the day by ringing the doorbell or telephoning.

JANUARY 28

While looking for a letter in my file cabinet this morning, I noticed a folder marked "Stress Course." Inside were papers related to a stress-reduction class Tom attended after suffering his first heart attack. When I saw his handwriting on a questionnaire, I became curious, and this is what I found:

Q. What are some things that make you feel good when you picture them in your mind?

A. Bev, home, my garden, my bees, a good book.

Q. What has been your most growing experience?

A. My heart attack and Bev's MS.

Q. What life experience stands highest in your mind?

A. Marrying Bev.

Q. What was the saddest moment in your life?

A. Hearing that Bev has MS.

At the bottom of the sheet was the following: "In my opinion, _____ is lovable; _____ is worthwhile."

Tom had written my name in the blank spaces.

Finding the questionnaire this morning was like finding a love letter from Tom in the mailbox. I read it over and over, crying, tracing his handwriting with my finger.

How lucky I am to have known such deep, tender love. The loss of it is what makes a rebuilding of my life so agonizing. I wish I could make others understand that, especially those who express a worry of how I am going to survive financially or how I am going to manage day-to-day living without Tom's help.

It isn't Tom's paycheck or his daily help that I miss. It is his love.

FEBRUARY 2

Tina went out early last evening, so I had supper alone. I lost my appetite the moment I sat down to eat. It had nothing to do with the food on my plate and everything to do with loneliness.

I turned on the television for company, but there was still an emptiness about the house. I picked at my food and cried. Then I reminded myself that all across the country there were other widows facing a supper hour alone and that many not only eat alone night after night, but live alone.

They have my admiration. I couldn't bear it. All my life I have shared living space—first with family, then with college roommates, apartment roommates, and finally with Tom.

I am sure it is an individual thing, but as for me, I like having another human being in the house. It is comforting to hear the sound of someone clattering dishes in the kitchen, talking on the telephone, moving about in the next room, or even running water in the bathroom. It simply means *life*, and oh, how I need that these days.

FEBRUARY 6

"The wound which causes us to suffer now will be revealed to us later as the place where God intended His new creation."

I found these words in Henri J. M. Nouwen's *Wounded Healer: Ministry in Contemporary Society*. I want to believe them. I want to have faith that God will indeed make of my grief, sorrow, and anguish, a "new creation," a new me. But doubt creeps in on a day like today when I am depressed and cannot dispel fear or gloomy, negative thoughts.

If I knew what the future held for me, I sometimes think, it would put my mind at ease. But I remember a day soon after the MS diagnosis when I felt the same way. "I wish I had a crystal ball," I said to Tom.

"No," he replied. "Even if it were possible to gaze into the future, it would be best not to."

Tom was right. If I had seen myself with a cane, then later using a wheelchair, and worst of all, facing widowhood, I would have lost all courage.

So I must remind myself that if I am to find peace, I cannot worry about the future. There is only today, the now, the moment, and I have to be patient about coming to the place where God intends His "new creation." Worry will not take me there, nor will tears and depression. Trusting in God will. It is a test of faith, and whether or not I pass is solely up to me.

FEBRUARY 8

Grief is a learning experience. I remember saying the words, "I am so sorry," to people whose lives were touched with loss, but I had no real sense of their pain. Their misfortunes were not mine. Their trials did not affect my life.

It is different now that grief has struck me personally. I still say, "I am so sorry," and I still mean it as sincerely as before, but I know some of the words beyond that phrase that will bring comfort, and when to say them. I remember the ones that comforted me, both in the immediate days of my sorrow and later—especially later, when the shock stage had run its course.

And I know that the reason for grief need not match my own. I have watched Tina as she works to recover from a broken relationship with the boy she was dating on a steady basis. Just before Christmas, Joel decided he no longer wanted to see her.

To Tina, it was like a death. She was shocked and even used some phrases I had used when Tom died. "I can't make it real," she said. "I keep thinking it is all a bad dream." She found it difficult to be with couples, to listen to certain songs, to get Joel off her mind. My heart went out to Tina. I searched for what I hoped would be the right words to say to her, and the right time to say them. In the beginning, she needed to hear, "Yes, it hurts. Yes, it is all right to cry." Today she was ready for something else.

She came into my room to ask about the pink carnation we had salvaged from the dozen Joel had sent her the day before he ended the relationship. We had pressed it between the pages of a heavy book. "I was just wondering how it's doing," Tina said.

We looked. The flower was nicely pressed. "What should I do with it now?" Tina asked. I showed her a white lilac Tom had given me years ago. It was in an envelope at the back of the book.

As is often the case with Tina, she said nothing. But a few minutes later she was back in my room, asking if I thought the envelope in which she had placed her carnation needed a piece of Scotch tape. The wide smile on her face told me that she was all right, and that it was time to tell her that memories can be sweet, the pain will ease, and there will be other boys in her life.

FEBRUARY 14. VALENTINE'S DAY

As much as I try to keep my thoughts forward-looking, on special days I am easily carried to the past in a rush of memories.

When I settled down to go to sleep last night, my thoughts were of how Tom and I always secretly bought Valentines for each other, then hid them under something on our night tables so that when we awoke on Valentine's Day, we could exchange cards even before getting out of bed.

I missed all of that this morning, and the tears came. But

when Tina brought in my breakfast tray, my gloomy mood disappeared. Propped up against a glass of orange juice was a red envelope with my name on it. Inside was a Valentine that said, "What this old world needs is more nice people like you." It set me to thinking about the word "love."

In the days when Tom and I first realized that we were serious about each other, we tried to define what love was. Tom said he thought it meant "caring." In fact, before he felt ready to sign "love" at the end of his early letters to me, he signed "I care, I really care."

I like Tom's definition. It seems right not only for sweethearts, but for husbands and wives, family members, and friends, too. If you care when someone hurts, if you care when someone is lonely, if you care when someone has a problem, that is a measure of love.

I know the truth of this at first hand through Connie's daily phone call or personal visit, through Mary's ever-ready listening ear on days when I feel I am drowning in despair, through the understanding that comes from the Support Group, and through countless acts of thoughtfulness that flow from all directions.

So, as I looked at Tina's card (and the five others that came later in the day), I decided that just because Tom is no longer here to give me a Valentine and to love me, it does not mean that I am unloved. On the contrary, love surrounds me. I have a right to be sad on Valentine's Day, but not to think of it as having no meaning this year.

FEBRUARY 17

Tom's mother once told me that the day before Dad Gordon died, she had a dreadful argument with him. It was over something foolish on her part, she said, and she felt guilty because she had not apologized to Dad. "I cry about it every night," she confessed.

I tried to make Mom see that there was no reason for her to carry such guilt. "Every married couple has disagreements," I said. There was no consoling her, however. At the time I thought she was being stubborn and much too hard on herself, but now I understand.

Just as Mom was haunted by having left something unresolved with Dad, so I have been haunted by the fact that I did not spend more time with Tom when he was in the hospital. For months I have wondered how to shed the guilt.

Yesterday I decided that what I must do is to forgive myself. I pretended I was talking to Tom and explained how I felt. Then I wrote on a piece of paper ten times, "I forgive you, Beverly."

It seemed a useless exercise — until today. This morning I woke up free of the terrible monster "Guilt." I truly have forgiven myself. There is no reason not to. After all, I did not know (or perhaps I did not want to believe) that Tom was going to die. And he himself said, "Don't come." He loved me so much that he wanted me to save my strength for what was ahead. He even used his last breath to telephone and say, "I love you, Hon. Good-by."

I took a sure step on the path to recovery today.

FEBRUARY 22

Why for the past three days have I felt low emotionally, as if I had made no strides at all? Why are tears at the surface day and night — why such a deep longing for Tom? Perhaps it is tied to the fact that this is school vacation

89

week. I keep thinking of last year at this time when Tom was enjoying a break after having been back to his classroom on a full teaching schedule for over a month. He was doing well, he looked well, our hopes were high.

I seem to be carrying in my head a sort of countdown of the number of weeks Tom had left to his life a year ago yesterday, today, or tomorrow. I wish I had known how few there were. There are many questions I would have asked Tom, many things I would have told him, many days I would have spent differently.

This morning I thought how wonderful it would be if a lost loved one could come back for just one day. I would like to have Tom here to see how I am managing my life and to have him tell me of where he is now. But this afternoon I remembered Emily in Thornton Wilder's play *Our Town*. She was allowed to return to earth for one day and in the end found that she was happier not to be here.

It is the emotional ups and downs that make grieving so difficult. On the good days, I am filled with confidence and positive thinking; on the bad days, utter hopelessness. Most of the time it has nothing to do with whether or not I am busy. I can be totally involved with something and suddenly feel captured in such a wave of despair that it nearly drowns me.

FEBRUARY 26

When Ferris was here today, I asked her to recall once more her visits with Tom in the hospital. She told me again of the day it snowed and how she found Tom crying and saying it was probably the last snowstorm he would ever see.

"And I told you about the day he said he wasn't afraid to die," Ferris said.

"Yes, and that he was only afraid of the mess he would leave me in." I added, "But was there anything else?"

Ferris thought for a moment, then remembered another conversation about death in which Tom had said he knew there would be a few minutes of intense pain and then it would be all over. And that is what happened.

For such a long time I have visualized Tom in his hospital bed feeling let down, frightened and alone. But now I know he was all right. He had come to terms with his own death, accepted it, faced it courageously.

Perhaps death and birth are somewhat alike. A baby leaves the mother's womb and enters the outside world alone. At death, a person leaves this earth and enters a different plane of existence alone. There may be others around to give support and to witness either event, but in truth, at the very moment of their happening, both are solitary journeys.

MARCH 1

Connie and Nat left for Wales today and will be gone until June. Saying good-by was difficult and brought to the surface something I have learned about myself.

Ever since Tom died, I have a fear of losing people who are dear to me.

It is a fear that could easily run deep and keep me from making new friends and building new relationships. Every time I reach out to someone, a red light could flash inside of me to warn that love equals risk of loss, and loss is agonizingly painful, so beware and have no part of it. But I won't let any of that happen.

When Tina's relationship with Joel ended, she said, "It hurts so much that I'll never love anyone again." I tried to make her see that what she ought to think about is what she would have missed if she had not known Joel—the happy times and the way she was special in someone else's eyes, even if only for a little while.

That's how I feel about Tom. In spite of the suffering and sorrow that have come from losing him, I wouldn't have missed having him in my life for anything in the world.

The truth is that nothing is forever, and while I can hardly bear to think of losing anyone who is dear to me, I know it is bound to happen. People will walk in and out of my life for as long as I live. But I am willing to risk the sorrow that comes with loss in exchange for the giving and receiving of love. To do otherwise would be to cheat myself of things precious and meaningful.

MARCH 7

Today's mail brought a letter of acceptance and a check for the Christmas short story I have been trying to sell. I was excited, and my first thought was "Oh! I can't wait to tell . . ." I stopped before I said Tom's name. There was a sting of sadness, a longing, a realization of how much I miss the little things that were part of my life with Tom— the sharing of exciting news, the way he would look up from a book and say, "Hi, Mrs. G., I love you," a telephone call during his lunch break, an unexpected hug.

Much of the time it is indeed little things that tug at the heart. I once read of a woman who wept uncontrollably at the sight of her husband's umbrella ten years after he died.

Only another widow could understand that kind of weeping. Anything that represents a beloved lost mate can bring a wave of despair so strong that it is like being pulled under by an undertow. I felt it yesterday when the auctioneer was here to take from the basement Tom's skis, ice skates, bicycle, and carton after carton of things there is no point in my keeping. It was painful to make a list of each item that was carried off for one of Charlie's Saturday night auctions.

I cried when I went over the list again later in the afternoon. At bedtime, however, I was ready to look at the practical side. What reason is there to hold on to things I will never use? And more important, if my goal is to build a new life for myself, it makes sense to sweep away the old.

MARCH 11

Today, while leafing through a notebook in which I keep favorite quotations, I found something totally unrelated to the notebook's purpose. On a back page, in my handwriting, was a list headed, "Things I Would Do If Left a Widow." It said—

1. Wait at least a year before making any major change in living arrangements.
2. Get a dog.
3. Seek out a widow support group.
4. Write.

I have no idea why or when I made such a list. Perhaps someone I knew had suddenly lost her husband, or something I read prompted me to think about the possibility of my being widowed. At any rate, I know I made the list long before there was a hint of Tom's heart problem.

It is interesting to see how close I have come to following my own advice.

As far as living arrangements go, when it seemed

impossible to find someone to live in, I was tempted to sell the house and move into some sort of supervised-living facility because it is physically impossible for me to take complete care of myself. But now that things have smoothed out, I know that staying in my own home is best. It is small, practical, affordable, perfect for my needs. Above all, however, it is where I am happiest. These familiar surroundings bring Tom close and give me a sense of belonging at a time when I often feel lost and abandoned. Selling the house would have been a foolish and irreversible mistake.

The second item on my list surprised me. I don't know why I wrote, "Get a dog." I would love the companionship of one, but other factors outweigh that. I could not feed or walk a dog myself, and it would only lead to a whole set of problems I don't need. Several people have suggested that I get a cat instead, because they require less care. I simply have to admit that I am not fond of cats.

As for the third item on the list, there is a Widowed Persons Support Group in town, but the majority of its members are in their seventies, and for the most part the organization is a social one with its focus on planned entertainment. It seems too much like a senior citizens' group—there is nothing wrong with that, but it isn't for me. I am too young and, besides, I am not seeking to be entertained. Rather, I want to share feelings and explore in depth all issues of widowhood.

Perhaps there is a hint of direction in the final item on my list. "Write," it says, and I have indeed been writing, even if only a little at a time. Unlike anything else, the act of creating a children's poem, a short story, or an article insulates me against all pain and sorrow. It is a true escape, for I completely lose myself in the work.

MARCH 16

Mary went to a dinner party last night where one of the guests was a man whose wife died only a few months ago. He is already dating, and there is talk of remarriage.

Over and over again I hear such stories. I think men are more likely to date and remarry after losing a spouse than women are. Perhaps it is that they are used to being taken care of and instead of meeting the challenge of learning to shop, cook, and keep house for themselves, they put their energies into seeking a replacement for the lost mate.

And on the emotional side of things, I think men are less apt to allow themselves time to move through the various stages of grieving. Most males still grow up believing they must not cry or express worries and fears. As widowers, they hold back tears, bottle up grief, and refuse to give in to sorrow. But repressed grief will eventually explode, and if a remarriage takes place before grief has had its way, surely it could spell disaster.

All of this has set me to thinking about my own feelings on remarriage.

When Tom and I bought our wedding rings, we had the word *forever* engraved in them, and that's how I feel — forever married to Tom, in spite of "till death do us part." That doesn't mean I am enshrining him or dedicating myself to his memory. It is simply that my love for him goes on, and I am content to know that there was in this world one special man whose being was essential to my happiness and mine to his.

There are those who believe that to remarry after the death of a spouse is to say that your marriage was so happy you want once again to live in the married state. I disagree. My marriage was extremely happy, and for that very reason I have no interest in marrying again.

Recently I heard of a woman who has buried three husbands and at age eighty is now into a fourth marriage. Unlike those who admire and commend her as someone who really knows how to pick up the pieces and move forward, I see her as one who has, perhaps, taken one husband after another out of loneliness, one who does not know the meaning of deep love in marriage, and one who, over the years, never saw the challenge of widowhood, never recognized it as a time of being free to do more than she had ever dared to do, a time to stretch her wings and to serve others. She has not been moving forward, she has been standing still.

MARCH 21

I wonder if I shall ever be ready to go to certain familiar places again. Today I turned down an invitation to Vermont. The drive of little more than an hour would not drain me physically, but just being there would take an emotional toll. Tom and I fell in love with each other and with that exceptionally beautiful part of the world both at once, and my heart tells me I would be miserable in that setting now even for one day. I could not bear to relive tender memories by physically returning to the place where they were created.

The high school is another place that fills me with dread. Much as I would like to attend some of the concerts and plays there, I cannot face going into that building.

Tom would be on my mind every moment, and the memories would be painful. I would think only of the day he left his classroom to drive himself to the hospital emergency room, never to return again.

Perhaps when time closes the wound in my heart more tightly, I'll feel differently about all of this, but for now I am allowing myself the privilege of staying away from surroundings that bring only pain.

MARCH 24

Coming closer to the first anniversary of Tom's death, I felt a need today to look back at some of last year's journal pages. I am glad I did, for I have discovered something important.

I knew it had snowed a few days before Tom died, but I had forgotten the magnitude of the storm. It was, in fact, a blizzard, and the reason I did not go to see Tom on either of the two days just prior to his death was that I was snowed in and so was everybody else. I even spent the night of the storm alone because the traveling was so dangerous that nobody was willing to risk being on the road to get here. People were not really dug out until the third day following the storm, and that was the morning I rushed to the hospital.

What a revelation my journal entries are. What strength they add to the forgiveness I granted myself several weeks ago. What absolute absolution! I didn't let Tom down after all—it was the weather that kept me from his side.

What puzzles me about all of this is how it has escaped me for so long. Why didn't the events of the storm come to mind months ago? I have no answer except to say that strange things come from the physical, mental, and emotional stress of grieving.

MARCH 28

"Great sorrow, for whatever reason, is too painful to take in one bitter dose. It would overwhelm. And so we intake bit by bit, in tiny insights, in waves that our minds cannot tolerate for long."

When I found this passage today in Ruth Vaughn's book *My God! My God!* I thought of how torturous it is to grieve in stages. If it were possible, I would gladly take all the agony at once just to have it over with.

But it doesn't work that way. The slow plodding and the gradual absorption of the impact are necessary in grieving. It is Nature's way. The mind and body could not survive the "one bitter dose."

When I had surgery a few years ago, I did not spring from the operating table as soon as the last stitch was sewn and resume all activities. The surgeon did his part, Nature did the rest—slowly, day by day, week by week. And while a permanent scar marks the place of the surgeon's work, it is not that smooth line on my body that matters. What counts is the healing that took place.

Why should it be any different with my sorrow? Surely time will close the wound. (I have already seen evidence that it has begun to happen). And yes, there will always be a scar, but what I must think of is the miracle that lies beneath it.

APRIL 9

There is no putting today's date out of my mind. It will stay with me for the rest of my life. It is something I shall remember as readily as I remember my wedding date, my own birthday, and the birthdays of people I love.

Tom died a year ago today.

The days have melted into weeks, the weeks into months, and the seasons have come full circle. I have moved through them sometimes with despair, often with anguish, and always with a measure of loneliness. But I have survived.

Looking back, dealing with widowhood has been, in some ways, like dealing with multiple sclerosis. From the moment I heard the doctor pronounce his diagnosis of my condition, I knew that fact was fact and that I could not deny or change it. Then a long process of adjustment began. And it was indeed a process. Anger, fear, depression, disappointment, and frustration had to be met head on and conquered slowly, step by step. In time, I came to be at peace with the disease, even to the point of rarely thinking of myself as its victim. While it is still a part of me, I have adjusted.

And so it is with this condition called widowhood. From day one I knew that it was fact and that I could not deny or change what had happened. Again a process of adjustment began, and the emotions along the way were familiar.

Similarities end there, however, for I cannot say that I am at peace with widowhood, nor do I believe I shall ever reach the point of rarely thinking of myself as a widow. I doubt that any woman who has lost a beloved husband recovers fully and totally. Surely there is always a shadow of sorrow in her life. I am certain there will be in mine.

But at least I have made some measure of progress.

Progress even though there are still moments when I glance out the window at Tom's beehive, the fruit trees he planted, and the place where he once had his vegetable garden, and an inward ache says, "It can't be that Tom is gone."

Progress even though there are still certain songs I cannot bear to hear and certain places I do not yet have the courage to visit.

Progress even though without warning, a deep longing for Tom floods my body from head to toe, bringing a fear that I might slip back into the pit of grief and making my heart feel as fragile as an eggshell.

Yes, progress—"even though."

I have long felt an anticipation about this day. From the beginning, I planted in some small corner of my mind the idea that if I could get through the first of everything, whether it be a holiday, a personally significant date on the calendar, or the making of an important financial or household decision, I would be all right. Each was the ultimate challenge, each a supreme test of courage and faith. And while more often than not I met them clumsily and awkwardly, I managed to put them behind me without completely falling to pieces, and that gives me confidence for the future. No misfortune will ever challenge or test me as widowhood has. Whatever befalls me in the years ahead will seem as nothing in comparison.

This morning I reread some letters that were sent to me in those first weeks of raw grief a year ago, and as I come to this final journal entry I want to record what Jack wrote. As a pastoral counselor and long-time friend, he knew the right words to say, the sage advice to offer, the loving way to hand-hold across the miles. Here is what he said:

What you had was precious and tenaciously meaningful, and to have it vanish suddenly is to be devastated. There is no way of minimizing it and its effects, but somehow recoil and resiliency will begin to take over, and by the miracle of personality you will bounce back, at least for some distance.

While you have probably said that you did not know if you could stand any more, the fact remains that you can, in spite of the worst expectations and fears. Nobody will say that it is easy, but usually the process is fairly automatic. You will just keep on putting one hour after another, and the rough place will fall behind you, although the memory will give pain for a long time.

Somewhere in the depths of each one of us is an unquenchable will and desire to see things through, and so we do. Whether or not you have yet come to that place is unimportant, but that you simply have to let it happen is vital.

When I first read that letter nearly twelve months ago, the only part I found believable was the opening sentence. Today I believe the rest. Somewhere in the depths of me I have found the "unquenchable will and desire" that Jack so wisely promised I would.

On this day of summing up, it is clear that I have been not only on a journey through grief, but on a journey of discovery as well. I have found a "me" I was unaware of a year ago.

I did not know I could live without Tom. I did not know I could function as head of household. I did not know I could feel so close to God. And along with all of that, I have discovered many new dimensions of love.

Because love had been given to me as an abundant harvest from Tom, I thought I knew its complete meaning. I have learned, however, that the love born of cherished marriage vows, devotion, and a special happiness that flows between a husband and wife is only one of the many sides of that emotion. They all add up to "caring," but like packages under a Christmas tree, they come wrapped in different ways from different people.

It seems a blessing that my first year as a widow ends at this season of the year. All around there is evidence of promise, and just as the grass and trees I can see from my window show signs of renewed life, so do I. It is as if I have been in twelve months of winter with more darkness than light, more storminess than sunshine, and now I have come to my own spring, my own time of renewal, my own new beginning.

Some Books that Helped

Burton, Wilma. *Without a Man in the House*. Westchester, Ill.: Good News Publishers, 1978.

Caine, Lynn. *Widow*. N.Y.: Morrow, 1974.

_____. *Lifelines*. Garden City, N.Y.: Doubleday, 1978.

Kreis, Bernadine, and Alice Pattie. *Up From Grief: Patterns of Recovery*. Minneapolis, Minn.: Winston Press, 1982.

Kushner, Harold S. *When Bad Things Happen to Good People*. N.Y.: Avon Books, 1981.

Moody, Raymond, Jr. *Life After Life*. N.Y.: Bantam Books, 1975.

Morris, Sarah. *Grief and How to Live With It*. N.Y.: Grosset and Dunlap, 1972.

Peterson, James A., and Michael P. Briley. *Widows and Widowhood: A Creative Approach to Being Alone*. N.Y.: Association Press, 1977.

Pincus, Lily. *Death and the Family*. N.Y.: Random House, 1976.

Titlebaum, Judy. *Courage to Grieve: Creative Living, Recovery and Growth Through Grief*. N.Y.: Harper & Row, 1980.

White Eagle. *Sunrise*. Liss, Hampshire, Eng.: White Eagle Publishing Trust, 1958.

Yates, Elizabeth. *Up the Golden Stair*. N.Y.: Dutton, 1966.

BEVERLY S. GORDON is a native of Peterborough, New Hampshire, and both she and her late husband Tom Gordon were dedicated teachers in New England schools. After the onset of multiple sclerosis, she turned to writing as a career and out of it has come this, her first published book, as well as publication in several magazines including *Yankee*. She was educated at Becker Junior College and the Perry School (now Curry College) in Massachusetts, and at Keene State College in New Hampshire. "This book," she writes, "is not only for women who have lost their husbands, but for families and friends who are seeking a better understanding of the grieving process that is unique to widowhood."

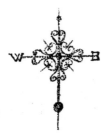

This book was typeset in Sabon with headings in Perpetua italics at A&B Typesetters, Concord, N.H., printed at the Transcript Printing Co., Peterborough, N.H., and bound at the New Hampshire Bindery, Concord.